DESIGNER BOYS AND MATERIAL GIRLS

DESIGNER BOYS AND MATERIAL GIRLS

Manufacturing the '80s Pop Dream

DAVE HILL

BLANDFORD PRESS
POOLE · NEW YORK · SYDNEY

To Laura Grace, with love

First published in the UK 1986 by Blandford Press
Link House, West Street, Poole, Dorset BH15 1LL

Distributed in the United States by
Sterling Publishing Co, Inc,
2 Park Avenue, New York, NY 10016

Distributed in Australia by
Capricorn Link (Australia) Pty Ltd
PO Box 665, Lane Cove, NSW 2066

British Library Cataloguing in Publication Data

Hill Dave
   Designer boys and material girls

   1. Rock musicians—Biography
   I. Title
   780'.42'0922   ML3470

ISBN 0 7137 1857 9

Typeset by Poole Typesetting (Wessex) Ltd

Printed in Great Britain by Mackays, Chatham

CONTENTS

ACKNOWLEDGEMENTS

As I discovered, sometimes uncomfortably, during the writing of it, this book is secretly my attempt to salvage order from a personal chaos of facts, fascinations, irritations and impressions not just about recent popular music, but the world at large. I never thought I would end up doing a job like this, and I'm very glad I did, because it strikes me that otherwise that chaos would be even worse.

So, in connection with my fortunate employment status I would like to say 'thank you, gentlemen' to Messrs John Fordham and Nigel Fountain, editors of *City Limits* magazine for enabling me to achieve it, and in particular to their colleague, Ms Penny Valentine, for being the first person whose opinion mattered, to tell me she liked my work. Such marvellous taste!

A number of press officers made material available for my research, most notably Barbara Charone, Rob Partridge, Pat Stead, Clare Smith, Versa Manos and Chrissie Cremore. In this respect I raise my hat especially to Mark Cooper at Virgin who found answers to a variety of tedious queries, and made much needed encouraging noises after ploughing through my first draft, as did my fellow scribe, Marek Kohn.

Much of the material herein is inspired by or adapted from articles of mine which have previously appeared in *The Face, The Observer Magazine* and, most regularly, in *City Limits*, but I am indebted to Paul Weller (candour) and Malcolm Garrett and Kaspar DeGraaf (enlightenment) for finding time to talk to me specifically for this project. Bouquets too for my agent June Hall and her assistants who stuck by the tome when fate played a dirty trick on us in the spring of '85.

On the domestic front, I've chewed my way through a vast number of biros during the construction of this work. The damage would have been far more serious without the invigorating mixture of inspiration and envy I frequently derived from three books: John Lahr's *Automatic Vaudeville*, Gerri Hirshey's *Nowhere To Run* and Greil Marcus's *Mystery Train*. Most of all, though, on the home front, love and gratitude to Nicki and baby Lol for regularly prompting and propping up a man who can often assume the temperament of a werewolf when he gets behind a typewriter.

Lastly, thanks to mum and dad for not giving up on me. Looks like I got there – somewhere – in the end.

Dave Hill
January 1986

INTRODUCTION
Free Market Farces

First of all, it's a question of cash. This is not because most of the *artistes* paraded in this book are millionaires – that, we expect. No, it is to do with a bigger idea of cash than that. It is to do with money being made, then thrown around, and then lost. Finally, it is about getting it back again.

A lot of things have changed since the strange and chequered culture of pop burst into the western world. With the boom years of the '50s came ebullient Elvis to personify burgeoning teenage lust. Through the '60s, the lovable moptop Beatle boys laughed, screamed and projected the beautiful illusion of a planet soon to be united in hope, peace and love. But by the middle '70s the dream boat was a floundering hulk as the optimism which affluence allows disappeared in direct correlation to evaporating assets. The music industry – the ultimate barometer of delicious falsehoods and hideous truths alike – began to feel a new and unsettling sensation – the Pinch.

The celebrity faces who appear in these pages are a product of the Pinch. Each embodies a different combination of the eccentric, the ridiculous, the despicable and the brilliant. Some proclaim themselves opposed to the thrilling elixir of stardom. Others are ready to die for it. But what unites them all is the knowledge that if you want to prosper in the galaxy of pop, you must do everything necessary to keep your star alight. They acknowledge the power of profit, that it's the movement of product which keeps all other ambitions afloat. Today's pop winner is a professional, an industrious cog in a newly-streamlined business machine that's busting a gasket to recapture its victorious past.

The new deities of '80s pop materialised from the fallout of the last great rock'n'roll blow-up – Punk Rock. Ever since the dawning of the economic slump, the music industry had been praying for a 'new Beatles' – some maverick but manageable talent to seize the mood of the moment, corner a vast, latent public consensus, and eventually, lucratively, *behave*.

Alas, Punk was not it. Punk did some magnificent things, a number of very stupid ones and whipped up a media frenzy like no youth cultural squib had managed for years. As a 'movement' it was nothing of the sort; but behind every triumph and disaster lay a single constant factor – Punk was irreversibly impermanent.

Beyond the white hot rhetoric, Punk's progress really *was* rock'n'roll's funeral march; a carve-up and a livid, delirious revolt into commerce. The Sex Pistols acted out the lurid conventions of outrage and hype with bare faces and immaculate technique. It wasn't so much *what* they were doing as the way they didn't give a hoot who saw them doing it. Previous rock revolutions had either concealed their greed behind the smokescreen of 'entertainment' or piously denied its existence. But with the Pistols there was no cleaned up front or moralist cant. They simply disported their destructive displeasure, took every cent from confused corporations they could, and gloated. Credibility was piracy without shame, and when the Pistols blew themselves ghoulishly to bits – fulfilling the consumer credo of built-in obsolescence – they completed a supreme display of market place theatrics.

For the industry, the Pistols' progress was too parodic a parable for rock and pop's hellfire transience to arrest its sorry decline; too incendiary by far. But how avidly they sought to absorb its scintillating sales pitch! Shoestring record labels like Stiff had keener eyes for talent and more smart ploys for promoting it than all the multi-nationals put together. Intellectual spivs like Sex Pistols manager Malcolm McLaren had whipped up a public fervour of the type corporate marketeers had hardly dared dream of, and his emergence as a pop role model to rival any performer is a sobering sign of the times.

So much for what is probably called the Conceptual Backdrop. Out here in consumer land, it all meant something dazzling and different. The rude new bands gave shape and expression to a new generation's degenerating inheritance. It was a very different one to that of the Baby Boom breed who had come to run not just the pop machine but most of the modern media as well. The oldest Punk era people were born at the back end of the '50s. By the time they were old enough to know or care what it was all supposed to mean, the Swinging Sixties had passed into history and its children into fashionable quasi-liberal careers.

The first wave of post-'60s adolescents had gazed at an altogether less confident bunch of stars – distant, mysterious people who dressed up a lot. At the ham end we got Glitter, but at the cool end there was Glam. David Bowie, Marc Bolan, Roxy Music, Lou Reed: these weren't rebel saviours blazing a trail into the virgin territory of Teen. For all their ostentation, they were fragile, intangible, more twilight than limelight in a way. They sang hymns not so much to the glory as to the *tragedy* of what Elvis Presley began. They weren't so much *of* rock'n'roll as *about* it.

Pop culture was the gift shop of the good times, but the Glams were a mutation; they emerged at a moment soon to be seized by doubt. Their response was vanity, irony, a flirtatious introversion. They were pop's first serious pessimists, and it was the people who bought their records who turned into punks. In part Punk transformed Glam's postulations into something unnervingly close to real life. 'No future', sang Johnny Rotten, and in so many ways he was right. The Pistols' horizons were inevitably limited, and even as they pronounced themselves the endpiece to rock's aspiration to constructive dissent, their final burn-out simply cleared the decks for the rise of a McLarenite phoenix. Punk had united rock'n'roll manners with a stylised sense of pop economics. With the former disgraced, the latter moved to centre stage. From now on, everything would be planned, programmed, pragmatic, and perfectly played out. We got pop with a brain in its head.

The '80s has seen the core of the pop industry define itself finally as *overground*. Pop culture sits proudly in the High Street with its sleeves rolled up and its fingernails clean. Among the cleverest artists, a consensus emerged around Pop as the ethos to adhere to. Pop implies a very different set of values to Rock. Pop makes no bones about being mainstream. It accepts and embraces the requirement to be instant, pleasing, and to make a pretty picture of itself. Rock, on the other hand, liked to think it was somehow more profound, non-conformist, self-directed and intelligent. Rock-think foolishly, innocently, imagined itself to be a bit above the manufacturing process. It refused to admit that it was a commodity.

Well, the people in this book know perfectly well that they are commodities. Not *just* commodities perhaps, but definitely up for sale. Pop in the past has always been denounced for being 'manufactured'. This fresh species of genuinely talented practitioners are ready and willing to *manufacture themselves*, capable contributors to the art of the sell. (Or is that the sell of the art? Or is there really any difference? Has there ever been?)

As the tendency took hold – and by 1980 it was dominant – new acts got a break, not by playing in scores of sweaty pubs up and down the land, but by creating little blueprints for swift (but massive) success. Once upon a time pretty boys and girls were bought up by businessmen, 'groomed' for shooting stardom, and forgotten. The sweet things of the '80s did most of the grooming themselves. They had a look, a philosophy and a public relations line as well as a handful of songs. Starlet and talent scout found common ground in the realm of *presentation*. Never before have commerce and creativity so happily held hands.

The most ubiquitous, expensive and absolutely crucial example is the promotional video. Without one, it is now highly unlikely that your single will become a hit. And that really says it all about videos, because videos are promos, and 'promo' is just a polite word for 'advert'. Secretly, videos are just moving hoardings, yet happy shoppers sally forth for a group's collected promo clips, and one of the newer bits of lounge entertainment tech combines video reproduction with top class hi-fi sound. Elsewhere videos are just accepted as free entertainment that is highly pervasive – in dance clubs, in pubs, in shops. Not, perhaps, so surprising in a culture where the TV ads are often watched more intently than the programmes they interrupt.

There is a sentimentalist argument that this great glut of day-glo visuals is a terrible con trick to make us look kindly on the dross in the records' grooves – part of the 'real music' argument, and sheer nonsense. Videos are just another part of something that's always been more than just music. At the same time, it's never been so much more than it is today. Modern pop – the phenomenon – is a huge, engulfing flood of magazines and books, memorabilia and merchandise, breakfast television, bedtime television, early evening television, television commercials, pin-ups, and chit-chat as well as audio discs. It is romantic to see the paraphernalia of packaging as just corporate flotsam obscuring the issue, because it *is* the issue. It's part of the message, part of the new pop dream, and each and every big golden fantasy face of today spreads its variation on that dream through every available channel; organically related elements in the immaculate sales conception.

Pop leads the charge as the media multiply, merge and compulsively cross-refer. In keeping with its escalating, almost rapacious profile around the world, today's western pop draws its inspiration from anywhere and everywhere, from books, films, art, across genres and, most importantly, across time. Poses, threads, and images as well as tunes are lifted wholesale, and the richest pickings have come from teen consumer culture's very own cast-offs. We witness a kind of romance dance with very recent yesterdays. We can't write it off as plain nostalgia, because the post-Punk people don't remember the originals. They receive them as displaced hand-me-downs; history as a junk dump reconditioned.

For each previous post-war generation there was a time before the youth market, a pre-Teen Age. The music and the mugs that defined it were symbols of escape towards exciting new rewards. But Punk said there were no new rewards, not anymore. So the Punk-era people decided to get practical. They took care of business, and in the absence of a future lived for the present and lived *off* the past. Since birth they'd been glued to the telly, plugged in to the radio, lost in the pages of tacky magazines, absorbing from their very first breaths, all that so seductive pulp that the Elvis industry pioneered.

The shop front of '80s pop is a collage of fabulous trash and cheap ephemera, refracted, reflected and painstakingly re-designed. The technological revolution is just gift wrap, a tool for putting the pieces of history together in whatever pretty patterns you desire.

The public seem to like it. The downward trend of record sales looks likely to reach a halt. There are no 'new Beatles', but there are lots of pocket versions, most of them from England, some from the USA, who together add up to a bright, clean, friendly, ultimately unpretentious Family of Pop whose members interact, move in and out of focus, like the characters of a soap opera. One minute the newspapers are devoting whole front pages to the sayings of Boy George, the gropings of Wham! or the snortings of Duran Duran. The next, they are united in their blessing of Band Aid – the soap's Xmas special – and Live Aid, its summer sunshine jamboree.

In the end nothing captures quite so neatly the pros, cons and preoccupations of the Born Again pop boom as that massive charitable effort which Bob Geldof – no bit part player in the overall production himself – initiated and hustled to fruition. At once a display of human goodness and a piece of philanthropic condescension, a helping hand for the cruelly deprived and a brassy exhibition of free enterprise heroism, Live Aid has become a life-line for crumbling western self-esteem; an article of faith. We create our Gods in *our* own image, not the other way round, and by the light of the Stars, we trip and weave our way out through the shopping centres and across the disco floor of life. The purpose of this book is simple enough: to describe and understand the smartest moves of modern pop's most fascinating favourites; and why it was we chose to make them what they are.

1

||||||||||||||||||||||||||||||||||||||||||||||||||||||||||||||||||||||||||||||||||||||||||||||||||||||||||||||||||||||||||||||||||||

THE POLICE
The Tale Of A Sting

It takes just one look into those vampire eyes to know that Mr Gordon Sumner always thought he was meant for better things. It took a long time and a good deal of compromise, but you can tell he finally believes he's got there. 'I just don't think about class any more, you know,' he explained when asked about his own upstart ascent from Geordie milkman's son to international sex bomb, 'I've been with the jet set. I've met Lady Diana and Prince Charles and felt equal to them. I just do not accept that I'm anything but equal.'

Mr Sumner, of course, rose to glory as Sting, the most prominent face of the Police, an extremely shrewd modern pop operation. They caught on early to the hard fact that pop in the '80s would be more to do with looks and lifestyles and product sophistication than innocent emotions or pretending to crusade for the rebel dream of Youth. The Police, with Sting as their elemental emissary, dispensed with this illusion, and replaced it with illusions of their own: musical, visual, intellectual – lots of them. The Police learned fast that pop was now a grown-up game, and they played it very well.

If Punk gave voice to the aimlessness of the first pessimistic post-war generation, then the Police were prime parasites of the new negativity. One of precious few consistencies in the movement's rag-bag of philosophies was the idea that you could do it yourself – with a handful of chords and a two-fingers attitude, you too could be a three-minute anti-star on the scene.

Buried deep beneath the layers of anarcho-speak, itinerant drummer Stewart Copeland, American abroad, recognised the glimmer of something lying at the core of his own family's soul – economic *laissez faire*. The son of a CIA bigwig, Copeland had been educated in England at the prestigious fee-paying Millfield school, and like many rootless restless rich kids, he'd channelled his energies into a recreation obsession – playing the drums. As a member of long-hair 'progressive' rock band Curved Air, Copeland had grown tired of endlessly contriving tours to pay off debts accrued during previous Curved Air projects, and in London's teeming punk scene he saw salvation: fun, an outlet for his competitive impulse, a manageable business operation on a small, but cost-effective scale which, the way things looked at the tail end of 1976, had every chance of becoming a big one.

A&M publicity shot of the three blondes which accompanied their '83 Synchronicity *album. After five years of success the image had hardly changed, a tribute to its appeal. Summers is on the left, Copeland on the right, and in the centre stands the world's most beautifully bleached human being.*

13

Sting was the dreamboat ingredient Copeland needed to transform theory into practice. He spotted him in the unlikely setting of a jazz-rock gig at Newcastle Polytechnic. Sumner was dark, bearded, but charismatic. He was also something of a musical snob, and his deep aesthetic feelings for high grade musicianship hardly coincided with the scene Copeland hoped to persuade him to take a free ride on.

There was, though, something else about punk rock that Sting liked very much. He freely volunteers that the Police used it as 'a flag of convenience', but nine years on, continued to declare 'an absolute faith in it as an energy. I really got off on this drive to destroy the music industry which had been trying to keep me out for years.'

Faced with a choice between tasteful North Eastern obscurity with his band Last Exit, and the vague prospect of fame through philistinism spurred by the drive of an enthusiastic American he'd never met before, Sting, already aged 27, took up Copeland's option. Packing up his then wife (the actress Frances Tomelty) and tiny son, he moved down to London.

Never, at any time, has it been the fashionable thing to align oneself with the manners, means and motivations of Sting and the Police. In 1977, as Punk raged through the tabloids and anything less than abject musical and emotional primitivism was marked down as heresy, to say you actually *liked* the Police was to carry some virulent social disease. Even today's Lifestyle People look down their snouts at them; but it was the entrance of individuals like Sting, Copeland and, crucially, his crusading brother Miles into the punk proceedings that put them where they've ended up today.

The Copelands were about Good Business. Sting is about Good Taste. Punk may have seemed like a weird environment for them to move in, but by 1980 Sid Vicious was dead, Joe Strummer was deadbeat and the Police had scored their first British number one. . .and that was just the start.

Good Business and Good Taste are what successful '80s people are all about, and the Police epitomised the deadly combination. It was Sting's adaptation of his own abilities and aspirations to the requirements of late Punk mass market chic that finally proved the key to charts and consumer hearts. A bass player, Sting had always been strong on self-improvement. Whilst attending St Cuthbert's Catholic Grammar School he would listen to avant-garde jazz albums by the likes of Thelonius Monk, not because he *enjoyed* them, but because he thought they would do him good. Gatsby-like Sting drove himself towards the higher things in life. 'I deliberately lost my accent very early because I didn't feel it necessary to use it. I've always assumed that I am actually really from the street, so it's not something I've particularly used. I'm not a working-class hero, but I am working class. There's something very pretentious and obvious about being a working-class hero. It just never appealed to me.'

Punk's celebration of crudity ushered in the concept of street credibility. But by the time the Pistols seized their piece of history, Sting's adolescence was long gone. For him, teenhood was about pruning those prole roots. In the old-fashioned way, education was his opening: 'I saw it as an escape. In the community where I was brought up nothing was expected of you. They wanted you to do well at school, but if you got a nice office job, that was enough. I think I was very bright as a kid, and I knew that there was an escape route, and it was through working well at school. It was through reading books. I did very well, both academically and as an athlete. An intellectual interest has always been with me, and was always encouraged at home. They didn't understand what the fuck I was on about most of the time, but they thought it was doing me good. I read *Treasure Island* when I was six.'

Sting's has been a journey from embattled isolation to the centre of the most exclusive stages. His entire career is infused with his lust for the *tasteful* life. And, through the Police, he has seen his ambitions realised with handsome interest.

At first, the group struggled. Though their line-up was completed by Henri Padovani, an archetypal punk guitarist (not exactly Segovia), their backgrounds meant they were excluded from the self-protective (not to say xenophobic) inner circle of London punkdom. But, helped by the entrepreneurial zeal of Miles, the group kept working, and a self-financed single *Fall Out* sold its first pressing of 2,000 copies. Then, when reforming '60s hedonist Andy Summers, a seasoned rock guitarist, replaced Padovani the Police really got on the case.

Summers' finesse allowed Sting to set the mark of quality on the group at last, and so created the turning point in the Police's transition from uncool bandwagon jumpers to one of the first acts catering to a mainstream market now ready to receive punky outlaws, as long as they were chic and polite.

In the time-honoured fashion, Punk's rhetorical spittle was already becoming diluted into a less volatile market solution – 'New Wave'. At the same time a media punk stereotype had been co-opted and it was with exquisite aptness that the three Policemen simultaneously confirmed and exploited this cartoon, by appearing in a TV advert. The Wrigley Spearmint Gum commercial called for shocking blonde 'punks'. Copeland already had the right colour crop. Sting and Summers dyed theirs for the occasion. With this Three Bleached Men look, the Police had a photo profile. With *Roxanne*, they had a song.

Written by Sting, *Roxanne* expressed everything that would be fundamental to their appeal. Melodic and deftly arranged, with a lyric about a man in love with a hooker, it was the work of experienced craftsmen rather than wild-eyed idealogues of social unrest – the type of construction Summers' skill made possible. Yet it possessed also the kind of sparseness, economy, and low-life flavour associated with the 'movement' they'd fed off.

The other vital ingredient was reggae. Punks and Rastafarians had formed a liaison of sorts, and the bass-heavy thunder of Jah music was enjoying a greater, and more respectable prominence in Britain than ever before. Stewart Copeland's adaptation of the form's revolutionary on-beat enabled the band to devise a hybrid of Punk's nervous urgency and reggae's engrossing pulse which they harnessed to the melodic conventions of pop. Pleasantly incongruous amidst their otherwise unspectacular protopogo sound, *Roxanne* excited the commercial instincts of Miles Copeland. He negotiated a deal with the major label A&M to release the song as a one-off 45. Banned from the airwaves thanks to the enduring double standards of BBC Radio One, and inadequately supported by both band (off on one of their famed shoestring tours of America) and company, the single didn't sell too well. But a lot of influential people liked it, including, ominously, Mick Jagger Esquire, and with it the Police broke the mould of Punk. It was the spring of 1978, and the Police's co-ordinates were set for the stars.

The public was ready for them. Punk was banged up and bought out, and attractions like Blondie and the Boomtown Rats had successfully made the transition from semi-credible 'punks' to 'New Wave' heart throbs. Sex Pistols were out. Sex appeal was in.

Blondie's singer, flower child turned trash-art paragon Debbie Harry, was the peroxide pin-up of stylised New York Farfisa beat: 'picture this, my telephone number,' she sang, and just about summed herself up. Meanwhile, the Rats' frontman, effervescent, articulate Bob Geldof had manoeuvred his way onto teenage bedroom walls, with a combination of traditional Irish charm, and heavy good looks.

15

These were the first of the overage teenies. Debbie wasn't an air-brushed, blow-dried kid from the cradle; she was past 30, post-Warhol. Geldof was no seething adolescent; he was in his middle 20s and had worked as a stringer for the *New Musical Express*. These people were their own shop-front tactitians.

Video was a crucial tool of the Boomtown Rats' trade, a dayglo framework from which they could project their irreverent but utterly affable personalities more vividly, more frequently and with more smartass sophistication than they could from a stage. In America, they were ahead of their time. Geldof tells a deliciously damning story of how a cassette containing a classic, giggly Rats promo was brusquely consigned to the waste bin by a representative of their Stateside record company – but in Britain they were blazing the trail. Actors, talkers, bright spark tunesmiths and huggable rogues, the Rats were their own PR unit, projecting their spikey showbiz selves through small screen and daily press. While the heavyweight rock papers loved to loathe him, Geldof got married to the then *News of the World* gossip columnist, Paula Yates; it was the perfect True Life love match for the new age of pop.

So Debbie was blonde, 'bad' and seductive and Bob was gorgeously dishevelled. The environment was right for Sting to join them as the Ace Face.

Although *Roxanne's* deft charm took the chill off the Police's cold critical reception – and this was a time when the *NME*'s word was law – it was Sting's step into moving pictures which truly defined one of the craftiest, most adaptable personas of these designer times. A bit part as an Eddie Cochran fanatic in Chris Petit's soporific art movie *Radio On*, had worked a treat. Now, with the success of Woking punk survivors the Jam helping to encourage a revival of '60s Mod culture among young metropolitans, the cult's early figureheads, the Who, were financing a film interpretation of their album *Quadrophenia*, a crypto-operatic piece about the phenomenon.

A part existed for a Mod-style paradigm – working-class, fastidiously turned out, and oozing ostentatious cool. Sting got the job, and although he barely spoke (perhaps more likely *because* he barely spoke) became the movie's figurehead. Distant, arrogant and desperately *clean*, he was an immaculate object. 'I have a very strong ego,' Sting told Nick Kent for the *NME* (1/9/79); 'in fact Ace is very, very much half of my character.'

The Ace role did indeed make Sting a Face, but defined only 50 per cent of a comprehensive public address based entirely on paradox and contrast. The second half of the Sting one-two was delivered with precision timing. *Quadrophenia* was premiered on August 16th, 1979. On September 7th, *Message In A Bottle* was released and swiftly topped the national singles chart, spurred by a second British headlining tour. The following month, the second Police album *Regatta de Blanc* – literally translatable as 'white reggae' – appeared in the shops. The entire product effectively etched in the flip side of Ace, and completed the arrival of Sting, career schizophrenic *par excellence*.

The *Regatta* product portrayed Sting as the personification of soulful vulnera-bility. *Message In A Bottle*, the album's promotional trailer, was the most potent realisation yet of a Sting compositional muse which characterised all his best early songs; crisp, melodic reggae-pop, topped with a sweetly pained falsetto voice, and a lyric about absolute emotional desolation. Perfect. When the LP emerged, its sleeve art redoubled the impression. Superficially it simply echoed the methodology of their debut, *Outlandos d'Amour* – three fair heads in a row. But where the *Outlandos* cover shot placed an abruptly coiffed Sting, scowling, stage left, *Regatta's* photo had him firmly in the foreground. The shade is a deep, moody blue; the singer's hair is longer, wispy, dreamy; he's a vision of aching sensitivity.

This dichotomy of Sting the razor-creased devil and Sting the soft-focus angel has become the trademark of his and the Police's international celebrity, and one which he has gleefully milked for all that it's worth. Certainly, he has proved himself eminently fitted for the part. Ever since that great leap into Fame, all the (intermittently) valuable things Sting has done have come out of this elementary yet immutably efficacious role.

The beauty of the Ace and his apparent direct opposite, the protagonist of *Message*, was that the archetypes could be combined as two polarised aspects of the same magnetic whole. The unfussy working out of the duality's contradictions informs all the decent songs Sting has recorded, and almost all of his very capable cinema appearances. In the Dennis Potter-scripted *Brimstone and Treacle* (1981) he starred as the central figure, Martin Taylor, a disturbed adolescent whose pristine looks belied a capacity for virulent, demonic malice. The same year he played in the bizarre, occultist TV epic *Artemis '81* as the Angel of Light, a character whose apparent goodness shed more shade on the baffling proceedings than sunshine. More recently, he's been cast as Machiavelli in the Arena presentation *Ligmalion* (all about conning your way to the top – such *fun*, what!), less successfully as the spiv innocent, Mick, in *Plenty*, and as the villain opposite Jennifer Beales in *The Bride*, an imagined sequel to *The Bride of Frankenstein*. He also got to play one of his favourite literary characters, Steerpike, in a Radio Four adaptation of Mervyn Peake's dense, dank, phantasmagorical *Titus Groan*, the first part of his acclaimed *Gormenghast* trilogy.

Sting's self-professed fascination for Steerpike is but the most obvious example of how he has inflated his own self-image in the name of entertainment and, crucially, *perpetuated* it. Young, resourceful, charming, and utterly ruthless, Steerpike slithered from his lowly position as a menial in the sprawling house of Gormenghast and infiltrated its upper echelons by a combination of stealth, flattery and deception. 'I've been living with that book for years, hoping to do something with it,' Sting confessed over posh Parisian strawberry sorbet in June, 1985; 'I even bought the film rights.'

Early sensitive Sting posture, featuring hooped T-shirt and chunky trainers. Behold the birth of the WASC -White Anglo Saxon Catholic – as captured by Pennie Smith.

If the Police were deemed tainted interlopers in the citadel of Punk, they outlived their credibility curse to become maestros of post-Punk ingenuity. By the start of 1980 they were ready to rule the world – an example for all who followed.

Softened musical and visual associations saved them from looking square, whilst the blossoming Sting factor sensualised the proceedings, *personalising* any threatening edges.

The singer's allure was now a refined and powerful thing whose ingredients included every fetished quality that now typifies the burgeoning Age of the Lifestyle. In the committed's mind's eye, Sting was a man who was fragile (his words, his highly-strung voice, the music's limpid mystique) yet decidedly humpable (his looks, the backbeat's compulsive pulse), and, of course, successful. Mr Mind and Body; Zen goes to Pineapple; one man, his torment and his torso. How could he lose?

Sting's writing provided the thrust of the Police's assault on the charts. Melancholic yet instantaneous, his hit songs were deliciously mopey and intimate. *Can't Stand Losing* (and how!) and *So Lonely* conformed to the same formula as *Roxanne* and *Message In A Bottle*, the track that cracked America. *Walking On The Moon* was spacier and cheerier, but just as dewily romantic, adding to the sense that Sting had not only learned the reggae beat from Jamaican pop, but owed a lot of his mystique to it too. There's a sense in which his posture is a European caucasian equivalent to the spiritual outlaw aesthetic which helped Bob Marley to internationalise his music. Sting even sang with a similar strained anguish, apeing Marley's vocal mannerisms and shouts. He did, however, lack a certain leonine righteousness.

The Police rose gracefully from the wreckage of Rock, reflecting changing times both artistically and as a business unit. 'I'd like to create a new archetype, of someone who's in control of what he's doing,' said Sting to *Rolling Stone* as the group began a remarkable fourth series of self-financing shows in smalltown America; 'an intelligent, thinking man. Most bands don't make money. They just squander it on producers and cocaine and lots of other bullshit, and it's disgusting. There's so much idiotic excess. It goes beyond enjoyment.'

For the Police, enjoyment was exploring the boundaries of their blooming international status. Already figureheads of recessionary survivalism, they became jet-setting crusaders for the new pop values. A world tour of unprecedented proportions took them to Canada, America, Hawaii, Japan, Hong Kong, Australia, New Zealand and most major European capitals, as well as to Egypt, Greece and India – places where modern western pop had scarcely been experienced in the flesh before.

For Miles Copeland all this was symbolic reparation for his faith in the Police and the American Way. A compulsive capitalist with a dreadful haircut and the very dubious appeal of the true zealot, Miles' most famous quote came after an early Police gig in Syracuse at which only four people turned up. One of the them was a local DJ who so enjoyed the band's maniacal set that the next day he played their records to death. For Miles Copeland this was more than a happy coincidence – it was a *sign*: 'That's why their success is such a tribute to their conviction,' he would later pronounce, recalling the incident; 'they'll play *anywhere* to *anyone*. They're prepared to do anything for success!'

Miles was more recently heard addressing the Federation of Conservative Students on the evils of socialism in particular relation to pop music, through which, apparently, the impressionable are now, unknowingly, assailed by some kind of deadly Red Threat. His most famous client, though, aspires to a more Fabian world perspective, liberally spiced with psycho-philosophical titbits from such thinkers as Arthur Koestler, Bertholt Brecht and Carl Gustav Jung. Perhaps Miles should have warned him about his dabblings with the giants of pink academia, since they have frequently contributed to his regular artistic cock-ups.

After their *Regatta* phase, we heard little of value from the Police till 1983 when they partially reverted to what they were best at – harmolodic pop melodramas in which Sting played himself. Their third album, 1980's *Zenyatta Mondatta* was made from the standpoint of adoration, completed under pressure, and bears all the predictable marks of harassment, contrivance and pretence. The leery single *Don't Stand So Close To Me* was a crass piece of self-congratulation of which all concerned should be deeply ashamed of. The following *Ghost In The Machine* (thank you, Arthur) saw the group trying to sidle away from the spotlight of teen and be terribly serious. Put together at the prestigious Air Studios on Monserrat, the entire effort was notable for just two things. One was the track *Invisible Sun*, which dealt, from an entirely non-partisan position, with the war in the north of Ireland. *Top Of The Pops* banned the video. The second was *Ghost's* complete and utter pseudery.

What we learn about the erstwhile Gordon Sumner, from *Zenyatta*, from *Ghosts*, from '83's semi-redemptive *Synchronicity* and from his first solo LP (*The Dreams of the Blue Turtles*, 1985) is that he's a lousy intellectual, but a much better Catholic.

'I don't regret it, my rather reactionary education,' he opined, just prior to *Turtles'* release; 'I was taught by priests. It gave me an awareness of spirituality, if you like. I spent my entire educational life with this crucifix of a tortured man bleeding everywhere. I suppose the guilt part, the heaven-and-hell symbolism is very rich, reactively. I'm still living in this medieval world of devils and angels,' is his reassuring conclusion.

The classic single *Every Breath You Take* with eloquent, unsettling simplicity, combined deep desire with a predatory edge. *Wrapped Around Your Finger* detailed the power struggle between a married couple that is the silhouette of love. The Godley and Creme videos for both hit songs came rich in celestial lighting and images of idolatory. The sacred meets the profane, and leaps to the top of the charts.

When he cuts out the theory and lets his feelings guide him, Sting can write songs which unpick the fabric of profound emotional conundrums. In all his public actions he marks himself apart from most of the new pop gang who've flourished in his wake. Unlike most of them, Sting is not guided by a subliminal nostalgia, and unlike Debbie and Band Aid Bob, the Police were not, in the end, a pre-punk model with New Wave knobs on. They were a steely new species and a very mixed blessing: artistically erratic, morally precarious, self-contained, deliberately enigmatic, in control and built to last. When he made his solo album, Sting got to play with the smart brand of jazzmen he struggled with in his youth. Just like Miles would have planned it, he got there in the end.

'People say I'm obsessive and driven,' he reflected, two days after witnessing the birth of his fourth child (and capturing the whole thing on video tape like a good Hampstead radical should), 'but it just seems natural to me to be that way. Every few months I learn something new. I've just got my licence for scuba diving in a very short time. I'm going to go diving in the Red Sea in the summer with the sharks, because it's the most dangerous thing to do.'

It's *conviction* entertainment all the way. Nowadays everyone wants to go swimming with the sharks.

2

WHAM!
Bad Boys Do It All Together

Once upon a time, we'd have assumed that pop stars like George Michael and Andrew Ridgeley had been invented by businessmen. Not any more. As well as being the incandescent smiles and soulful eyes of a million teenage daydreams, as well as providing the guitars and voices on a string of sizzling hits, George and Andrew were also the writers, dancers, designers, talkers and the *entrepreneurs* of their monstrous success. Wham was a showbiz concerto in which G and A were both the celebrity duettists and the conductors of the orchestra. They were sheer entertainment. They were the winsome twosome. Clean, cute and thoroughly accomplished Wham were, in all ways, perfectly formed.

George and Andrew didn't care what cynical people thought. Why should they? Put to them things that other stars liked to deny and they would cheerfully concur. Yes, they always wanted to be famous. Yes, the big idea was always to turn into pin-ups. Yes, they liked the idea of being universally adored. Who wouldn't? It's only normal, isn't it?

From their early teens as bosom buddies at Bushey Meads school, Watford, George and Andrew had dreamed of making it big, of being good at this pop star thing. When their manager Simon Napier-Bell first saw them on *Top Of The Pops*, one of the qualities he liked about them most was their poise, their keen sense of presentation. 'I know exactly how *Top Of The Pops* works', he would later explain, 'and they looked as if they'd been directed and positioned with a care that the programme doesn't give to *any* artist. They must have worked the whole thing out themselves and forced it on the director.' Wham came prepared. They'd been waiting for this for years.

George and Andrew were nice, polite, classically middle-class suburban school boys who liked having fun. Pop was an important part of the scenery. Playing around at each other's houses, they'd compare notes about the ups and downs of the singles chart. Their favourites were ham glam purveyors of spangled camp outrage; moderately talented comedians like Elton John and Queen; tarts in platform boots with a flair for showing off.

And for the future boys of Wham, this was the stuff life was made of. 'If I went through life thinking it was a serious business,' George explained at the back end of '83, before the big time had really come their way, 'then I couldn't really be escapist. So I prefer to think of life as something I'm going to go through having the best time possible.'

Dorothy Lamour and Bing Crosby on the road to eternity, Xmas '84.

When the Whams first popped onto the scene in the summer of '82, they caused a little *frisson* of surprise. With their song *Wham! Rap!* they said what was publicly unsayable – that being unemployed was *nice*. The message was their market hook. Hello to Soul On The Dole.

Wham! Rap! became an anthem for a new ideology in pop. It was a song about not having a job which actively celebrated the fact. The wicked Whams trilled that a life of enforced leisure was something to be glad about. Thus Wham planted themselves firmly at the 'street' end of a set of attitudes which have since come to characterise the most smug, fatuous and odious of those self-styled 'social commentators' who have rendered the upmarket Sunday newspapers insufferable. At the time though, *Wham! Rap!* did not sound like the march of the Lifestyle people. Rather, it impressed as an act of defiance targeted at both the 'on your bike' brigade, and the pious patronage of the professionally 'concerned'. With Giro in hand and a head full of scams, the Good Life could be yours.

Wham's offering was a lightweight wafer of funk, a brash, bubbling offering which worked equally well on the radio and the dance floor. This was a bubblegum version of the clubland music which George and Andrew had always enjoyed, of a culture which was now, after thriving in the twilight for over 20 years, becoming dignified as a philosophy of life. *The Face* magazine did it in its glossy pages; Spandau Ballet did it in interviews; and Wham set it to music. It was the perfect pop ploy for an age of retrenchment, and bore the seed of a blend between dissent and conformity so subtle, it could be consumed as either or both.

The Wham manifesto was simple but seductive, and Mark Dean was the first to spot it: 'What we signed was two guys who, OK, were middle class, but they had a rebellious streak in them. They wanted to be the English versions of . . . I don't know, Prince or something. George in particular had a lot of charisma. He wanted to be a bit of a James Dean character, a bit of a rebel.'

At 20, Mark Dean was just one year older than his dashing protégés. He had already proved his prowess as a talent scout at Phonogram for whom he had signed ABC, one of the first, wittiest and best of the new generation of conceptual pop acts. As a result, CBS moved in and set him up as head of a licensed label, Innervision, effectively a vehicle for Dean's flair. When George and Andrew turned up, their assets were two pretty faces, a nice line in chat, and a cassette with one and a half songs on it.

One of these, *Wham! Rap!* was put together in the studio by Bob Carter, the best-known producer in the UK soul field having honed hits for Junior Giscombe and Linx. The song was a shrill Anglo-Saxon reading of the heavy duty Bronx rap records which had been crossing the Atlantic of late, but *Wham! Rap!*'s was the gospel of imminent success, not the interminable pressure of the ghetto. In photographs George and Andrew relaxed in the sunshine or threw ostentatious dance-floor poses, dressed in casual strides, squeaky slip-ons and crispy clean shirts. From trim coiffure to continental soles, the message was clear: no fights, no frowns, no trainers or jeans – disco dreamland here we come.

Wham! Rap! didn't make the charts, but it generated plenty of interest. With their initial mark made, Wham only needed a similarly insistent follow up to break into the Top Forty, and *Young Guns (Go For It)* – song titles with brackets were very much a *soul* thing – fitted the bill. Once more light-fingering the rap tendency, *Young Guns* etched a true life scenario of a different kind – stripling braggadocio reels as best buddy announces switch to hitched marital status. But in the song's final verse, the boy heroes get back together again.

The song was a turning point for Wham, and not just because it went all the way to number three in the singles chart. The vital thing was that the Unavailable

Couple had arrived. It was this chemistry, this unspoken, enigmatic relationship between the two, which defined Wham's special fascination for a nation more obsessed than ever with the private habits of public personalities. George and Andrew – two men . . . together! – were a fresh and titillating combination as Simon Napier-Bell and Jazz Summers, his partner in the management company Nomis, were swift to appreciate when they watched the duo act out their mini-macho melodrama on TV.

'We both agreed that they were without doubt the most vital and interesting group we'd ever seen,' explained Napier-Bell to *City Limits* just before Christmas 1984 – the end of his second year of minding Wham's affairs; 'what I saw immediately was this fantastic image which has been the basis of the film industry throughout the century. That is, two guys – two *straight* guys – who care more about each other than they do about the girls. During the film one of them might fall in love or go off to a brothel or whatever, but at the end, they ride off into the sunset together. It's the sort of macho, homoerotic image that's never been used in pop. I was certain it would be one which everyone would latch on to.'

It is surely the most adaptable profile of the entire new pop crop to flower in the aftermath of Punk. Their devotion to each other set against their loudly professed heterosexuality amounted to the classic, elusive arrangement for tormenting teenage girls. For budding young men, meanwhile, Wham offered an irresistible fantasy self-image. Those wooed by the flattering photos and ebullient beat found the exclusivity of the friendship totally tantalising. What *did* they talk about? What *did* they get up to together? What succulent secrets did they share? This was a teasing kind of rebelliousness, based on independence rather than aggression or subversion. Their manners and looks were flawless and sanitary, so parents could approve of them too. In short, George and Andrew were young, free and single . . . and one delicious fraction out of reach.

As their individual characteristics became inflated in the media spotlight, so the magnetism of the relationship was compounded. George was the singer and wrote most of the songs. He was the confident one who did all the talking. Andrew, guitarist, was the quiet, doe-eyed, soulful half. It hardly mattered what happened to or between the two of them. Every incident would just be perceived as another thrilling episode in the story of their lives. 'It's just like Burton and Taylor,' glowed Napier-Bell; 'If they have a huge row, get divorced and throw things at each other, it's just as commercial!' And, as history shows, he was right.

Even a legal battle which prevented the group releasing a record for some six months added to the sense of saga. Once signed up to Nomis, Michael and Ridgeley's contract with Innervision came under scrutiny. Wham had approached the company in December 1981 and inked an agreement worth a somewhat minimal advance of £500 apiece. A dispute ensued. Napier-Bell has described the agreement as 'an appallingly bad one.' Mark Dean, whose label had added a hit by Jimmy The Hoover to the achievements of Wham, looks back and bemoans the entire episode. Innervision had taken 2.8 per cent of the market for singles in the UK, an outstanding performance for a minor label.

A re-issued *Wham! Rap!* gave George and Andrew a second hit. And as *Bad Boys* – the silliest variation on the theme they would manage to contrive – completed the hat trick, the group commenced a short domestic tour to promote their forthcoming debut LP. Nomis helped hustle their charges into the bosom of Fleet Street. They've been there ever since.

'Initially we had to do an enormous job with the press to ensure that they gave them the sort of coverage which hadn't been seen even with Culture Club, and probably since the Osmonds,' revealed Napier-Bell to *City Limits*. 'That was important while we were in litigation, so that CBS were more aware than ever that they had a major group; so that they couldn't say "oh, they're too much trouble".'

The tabloids are now *the* crucial print medium in the launching of a pop phenomenon. And while the legal wrangling went on behind the scenes, Wham shook their tennis shorts at the cameramen – raising the stakes a little higher with each candid exposure.

Innervision went to court and won a temporary injunction against Nomis. But Wham finally signed with CBS after an out-of-court settlement. 'The boys needed things we couldn't deliver,' is Dean's rationale for the whole affair. 'We needed things from CBS to help us out which *they* wouldn't deliver because they knew it gave them leverage to get the band in. In the end it was a bit of a muscle job, but what can you expect? That's the kind of business I'm in.'

Whatever the rights and wrongs, a bit of muscle doesn't hurt in this game, either in the back room or the shop front. Wham had vigour, enigma and firm young flesh. They let the public have a look at it.

The sleeve to their 1983 album *Fantastic* offers pure Bad Boy posture. They gaze out at us with immaculate mannered moodiness. Beneath their leather biker jackets, hanging recklessly open at the front, we see their tanned and yummy torsos. Braggadocio meets Boystown in a tumult of Born Again Teen! *Fantastic* introduced us to a sparkling Wham world of beachwear, bare bits of body and neat little bottoms. It was all too much.

The album carried all three hits among its contents of eight, a version of the old Miracles hit, *Love Machine*, a breathy, morning-after lament, two bits of spring-heeled fluff-funk and . . . *Club Tropicana*.

Club Tropicana ushered in a new phase in Wham's climb to glory. It defined the image that would accompany them to international fame of stupendous proportions. *Fantastic*'s inner sleeve carried a clutch of Polaroid snapshots of the boys loitering, sleeveless, on the sand, and on sunlit streets. The message was that holidays are best, and *Club Tropicana* was George Michael's paean to an Ambre Solaire existence.

For critics who'd warmed to *Wham! Rap!* as heralding a new wave of dancefloor disobedience, *Fantastic*'s narrow insubordination (anti-parents; a Jimmy Dean hand-me-down) and hymns to fantasy escapism signified The End. Sweltering George urged our abandonment to a night-life fantasia (based on Le Beat Route club in Soho) where celebrities lay deeper than August Darnell's turn-ups, and encounters with ecstasy could be yours at the touch of a stranger's hand. Phew.

Scandal! The critical squabbling which accompanied *Club Tropicana* provides a dream illustration of what had come to divide the rock commentators of the old school from the pop reporters of the shiny full colour papers whose circulations were outstripping them. Over in *Smash Hits* territory Wham continued to be coddled and cosseted because that's what *Smash Hits* territory exists to do. But in *NME* land, the Whams' latest effort was instantly denounced as the sound of selling out, thereby showing how the 'serious' papers had a tendency to aid and abet their – otherwise inevitable – circulation crises during the rise of the so-called 'new pop'.

In truth, there was no discrepancy between the messages of *Wham! Rap!* and *Club Tropicana*. Rather, the second simply posited a wished for fulfilment of the hopes inherent in the first. *Club Tropicana* was written *before* George and Andrew had a recording contract, and so can hardly be attributed to the emasculating tendencies of accumulated cash. 'Wham! Rap! (Enjoy What You Do)'. In *Club Tropicana*, the drinks were free. Both songs were right in line with the twosome's plainly stated *raison d'être*: the pursuit and capture of the Good Life.

Wham were already masters of the marketing method. Their every word, note and posture contributed to a formulation of signs, cyphers and symbols which rejected the metaphors of boredom and strife, replacing them with the wonderful dream of plenty. Together they implied an image of a life beyond work, mortgages, long-term commitments. All the public had to do was colour the fantasy in.

Monetarist times have come steeped in the fraudulent fragrance of yesterday, and the Wham operation contained all the necessary assets to mix modern world infatuations and rosy visions of a classic pop past into a heady cocktail of contemporary creative commerce. Though from different generations both the artists and their manager shared the same eclectic perspective.

Simon Napier-Bell first became involved with pop back in the Swinging Sixties when he co-wrote the English lyric to an Italian ballad and gave Dusty Springfield a hit with *You Don't Have To Say You Love Me*. He subsequently became manager of the Yardbirds.

In those days, it seems, people got a slice of the new young, allegedly classless action almost by accident. 'In the '60s,' Napier-Bell told *Him Monthly* (Jan '84 edition), 'I was bluffing, I was learning. Now, I *know* the business.' The roller coaster of British affluence which gave life to the culture of pop offered a free hand to the buoyant momentum of its stars; big cars, big homes, big egos, big debts. In the '70s, everyone started paying; and in the chastened '80s, air-conditioned, shrink-wrapped lifestyle shopping seals us off from the underlying despair. People want their trivia finely tuned and the competition is hot. 'When this kind of thing happened ten years ago,' George Michael noted, 'it usually happened to people who were being written for, and who had no particular desire to make anything other than totally disposable pop records. But although ours are disposable in that they are pop records, we, and the other screamed-at groups of the moment, have a lot more class than the teenybop stars of before.'

Wham worked like crazy to make people think they were lazy. Behind the suntans lay the sweat and toil of self-improvement. For all their early dole boy irreverence and jokey street cred assertions, the Wham! boys' backgrounds had steeped them in the very same middle-class skills and business acumen which informed a new breed of Parliamentarians successfully exploiting recessionary neuroses in the House of Commons.

'I think one of the things our first record combatted was apathy,' said George; 'the kind of apathy which is seen as being inevitable. But the truth is that kids have got more money than ever. The fact that there is no work is definitely a problem, but if you tell people this from the age of ten, they're not going to believe in anything or strive for anything. If you still want to make something of yourself, I believe you can, in whatever field. You just have to have ambition.'

Wham's was a revolt into pleasure, an escape into consumption. As their celebrity grew, so reality increasingly matched their fantasies. 1984 progressed, and George and Andrew became abstracted figures, media creatures, shiny pop stars in the old untouchable mode. Pop in the early '80s had seen its creators flirting with the clichés of stardom. Wham were different. They played it absolutely straight. The last phase of their career looked like a re-run of the archetypal pop dream. There was no underlying irony; only the context was different. And the whole point with Wham is that context shouldn't interfere with the fun. That's the bottom line with the Fake Swinging Sixties – this time only half of us think it's real.

George Michael was now writing all the songs, and began severing ties with the funk grooves which had inspired the first Wham compositions. He turned instead towards '60s pop artifice. *Wake Me Up Before You Go Go*, the comeback Wham single after the legal battles had been resolved, breezed along on a kind of saccharined R&B backbeat. Michael delivered it with a glutinous, almost Eurovision dash of superficial ecstasy. The song's big, bounteous chorus leant it an air of free-wheeling euphoria. The video featured a bronzed Mr Michael in his Choose Life T-shirt, grimacing, pouting and flouncing his streaky new bouffant hairdo. *Wake Me Up* roared its way to number one in the UK.

The song was the first Wham release on the Epic label, sister company to CBS. Now they were fully tied to the multi-national conglomerate, it offered them the long-awaited chance to gain on their rivals who were cleaning up on the other side of the Atlantic.

The British teen pop press had voted George and Andrew their third favourite pin-ups at the end of '83, trailing only behind Culture Club and Duran Duran. Yet while Simon, Boy, and the rest of the gang were spearheading the Born Again British Invasion, Wham meant nothing to Uncle Sam.

Selling the group to CBS in the States was the final part of Nomis' three-part plan to catapult the tanned ones to the top around the world. When *Wake Me Up* made it to number one over there as well, it was the culmination of six months' solid arm-twisting. 'American companies are cynical way beyond the level of English ones,' Simon Napier-Bell explained. 'They are disinterested, and afraid for their jobs. For them, it's safer *not* to try to "break" a new record, and so not get fired for picking the wrong one. So you really have to pressure, nag and pressure, and get other people to pressure. That's where clout comes into it. That's where power politics come into it. You finally force them into a position where they have to deal with you.'

The group's conquest of the Land Of The Free, in tandem with George's stylistic changes, helped fuel the media's lust for promoting new approximations of glittering by-gone British eras. The 'British Invasion' was perfect, off-the-peg reminiscence to set alongside the royal births and the Falklands war. Why, George Michael was even beginning to look like Princess Di, and what a thrill it gave us to see our pop boys putting it across the Yanks again!

For the fresh-faced, all this was shiny and new. For the over-40s it was a subliminal trip down Memory Lane.

As 1984 rolled on, the struggle for supremacy among Britain's pop aristocracy moved towards an epic Christmas climax. The Whams, the Spands, the Boy and the Frankies bitched and bounced around the charts. In August, Frankie Goes To Hollywood's thunderous *Two Tribes* whipped *Wake Me Up* from the top spot, and stayed there for nine weeks. It was finally displaced by *Careless Whisper*, the first solo single by George Michael.

Aside from selling an awful lot of records – 750,000 in five weeks, which outstripped all the Wham releases – *Careless Whisper* opened up another breathless chapter in the tale of The Friendship. Was George going solo, shock?! Aside from a joint writing credit for Ridgeley, the single had no contribution from the other half of the team. George appeared on the cover of the *Sunday Times Magazine*, modelling a Hawaiian shirt, smouldering for all he was worth. His social doings were documented in every gossip column. He even got his photo in the gay press, holding hands with disco drag queen Divine. Would the little girls understand? What about poor old Andrew who preferred to stay at home?

Wham-to-split speculation successfully fuelled the rumour industry well into '85, guaranteeing the delectable duo's pre-eminence after their return from a compre-hensive world tour, right up until their historic trip to the Peoples' Republic of China. Even without a record the pair made the cover of *TV Times* ('The Truth About Wham!') as well as competing pop glossies *Smash Hits* and *No.1* in successive weeks during March. 'Wham To Split?' squealed the former, on the basis of a bare half page of hurried quotes containing sundry indications of a certain weariness, but

Innervision publicity photo which accompanied the duo's lauded debut 45 Wham! Rap! *Its appearance marked the first investment of critical credibility in slip-on casual shoes.*

not much else. 'George and Andrew's Solid Bond' piped IPC's rival seven days later. Take that!

From the *Mirror*, we learned that readers had voted George's trim hindquarters 'Best Bottom' of 1984. From breakfast television we discovered that George had purchased the 20-bedroom luxury Surrey home that had belonged to the late glam camp icon Diana Dors. From the pages of the *Evening Standard*, Mr Ridgeley's model girlfriend informed us that Andrew's was the perfect mouth to kiss. From the cover of the *Sun*, we heard of 'Randy' Andy's alleged indiscretions at a rugby club disco. 'Drunk Wham Star In Sex Row' screamed the headline of the soaraway one. George and Andrew were in danger of becoming The Queen And Prince Andrew Mk II! 'These days they make up stories about Wham every day because they know it sells papers,' said Simon Napier-Bell with the air of a man whose holy grail would never again be wrested from his grasp.

Wham earned this preposterous press saturation because they won the great Christmas Sales war of '84. All the biggest names had product in the pipeline at $33\frac{1}{3}$. Record companies plotted and spied, anxious to avoid sharing a release date with one of the others. Frankie's *Welcome To The Pleasuredome* was a strong favourite, having made history with advance orders of over a million. Culture Club, who'd been the talk of America (Joan Rivers and all) and had wooed the youth of opulent Japan, made ready with *Waking Up With The House On Fire*. Duran Duran kept themselves visible with a double live set, *Arena* (recorded round the world!), topped up with a pair of television specials.

Wham, with the perfectly entitled *Make It Big*, seemed to be outsiders. Yet, by the end of the year, it was clearly they who had the staying power. Frankie, poetically enough, came too soon. Culture Club simply disappointed. The Duran effort, being basically old material, was of limited appeal. But, gee'd up by the trailer single *Freedom* becoming yet another Wham number one, it was *Make It Big* that Santa had to hoard most of during the final seasonal sales rush. Meanwhile, the duo's special festive single *Last Christmas* (written whilst watching *Match Of The Day*, George told a tabloid newspaper), backed with yet another track from *Make It Big* (*Everything She Wants*) was kept at number two only by Band Aid's *Feed The World*; and George, of course, contributed a polished verse to that as well.

Make It Big was a famous and vindicating victory for Wham. The components of their triumph proved how comprehensively suited they were to exploit pop's burgeoning status as the nation's spiritual solution to everything from drug addiction to world starvation. The album was a softer, less excitable treat than the previous one, affording easier access to the over-18s. The starlets' image too was more mature, as befitted two high-spirited but free-enterprise-literate young men who'd now moved into their twenties. The leather posture gave way to cooler weaves, and subtle shades of coffee creme.

These progressions were yet further testament to the seeming inexhaustibility of the duo's pretty market profile. By the end of 1985, a year in which many of the noisiest names had taken to hibernation or retreat, Wham were still topping the chart with an off-the-wall festive knees up, *I'm Your Man*. And when at the same time George was seen painlessly accompanying his adolescent idol Elton John on the madly macho *Wrap Her Up*, it proved that there is no way that Boy George or the Frankies can 'age' in so conventional a way. *Make It Big* also confirmed beyond doubt George Michael's prowess at all aspects of contemporary commercial creativity. Just as he sprawled, crimped, preened and perfectly pressed, into the foreground of the album's cover shot, so he sprawled all over its contents. Of eight tracks, George had written six on his own. Ridgeley's only composer's credit came on *Careless Whisper* which had been co-penned before their days of fame (and which could apparently be legitimately portrayed as a group composition if it meant filling up the vinyl more easily. In America too *Careless Whisper* went out under Wham's name as a single). A cover of the Isley Brothers' *If You Were There* completed a set, of which half either had been, or shortly would be available as 45s, and almost all of which proved George Michael to be, in the words of his manager, 'a brilliant pastiche songwriter'. Slush, pop, and synthi-funk, all of it immaculately crafted and produced (by Michael, of course), there was something here for all the family. The complete modern pop performance.

Simon Napier-Bell is a man who knows what his clients are worth and is more than glad to promote them: 'George is a consummate writer of hit songs. He *knows how to do it*. The others don't particularly. Frankie have it done for them,' he continued, inspecting his nails (and rather bending the truth), 'and George of Culture Club has shown absolutely that the hit songs he wrote were lucky. Now that he has decided to be genuinely creative, it's clear that the stories one hears about him going into Virgin with three Diana Ross albums, taking the chorus of one song, the verse of another and putting them together, are true.'

A catty remark, but Napier-Bell's trumpeting on his charge's behalf is not without an element of truth. Even George's pals-for-the-day at the Band Aid recording session had to grudgingly admit that the blow-dry boy wonder sang better than anyone. Indeed, Michael has all it takes to thrive at the top. He possesses the fraudulent panache of a game show host, and a writing knack worthy of Tin Pan Alley. Where others revamped the Pop approach as partial parody, Wham played the game straight and in strict sympathy with the classic rules. Fatuous and facile they may have been. But, unlike their contemporaries, Wham really *were* less than twenty at the start. They ended up as the new and Total Tycoons of Teen; the genuine article, no less – you just can't argue with that.

3

||||||||||||||||||||||||||||||||||||||||||||||||||||||||||||||||||||||||||||||||||||||||||||||||||

EURYTHMICS
Don't Touch

Glam means never having to say 'I will'. It means you can intrigue and attract, but keep your options open. It means you can be – or *appear* to be – both icy cool and raging hot. Glam is a complex and powerful state of ambivalence, and Annie Lennox epitomised its emphatic '80s re-birth.

In the course of 1983, Eurythmics, the duo of which Lennox is the singing half, soared to the pinnacle of first British, then American pop. They did it with the song *Sweet Dreams (Are Made Of This)*, and within the story of its resonant success lie crucial clues to the nature of Glam's multitudinous dichotomies, and also to the very soul of British pop. It wasn't just the melody or the lyric – both are intriguing rather than thrilling in their own right – but the *idea*, and how it was delivered, which made *Sweet Dreams* and its creators something special.

Take it to pieces and the song is a mesh of coolly opposed contradictions. Lennox's voice is liquid, swooping and clear, but it also has a distant quality. The melody is lilting but disciplined, driven by rhythmic electronic undulations, and garnished with swathes of synthetic symphonics. The effect is somehow both austere and desirous, and the song's full title comes across more as an uncertain enquiry than an assertion. What's more, the artists didn't answer the question; they simply acted out the dilemma.

The symmetries of the record found echoes in every other dimension of the product's presentation to the world. Dave Stewart, the synthesist, co-writer and co-producer of the track, also devised the promotional video which accompanied it. The award-winning clip set images of technology against images of nature. A cow appears in an office complex. A home computer pops up in a cow field. A query is implicitly made through what is a blunt but effective stunt. Did this ever cross your mind? Can such things co-exist? Sweet dreams are made of *this*? And, to redouble the impact, the entire conundrum came focused squarely in both the voice and the persona of Ms Lennox herself.

What a star she was. What a *hairdo* she had! There are full grown legends about Annie Lennox's hostile coiffure, the one she wore on the way to fame. It was a splendid shock to witness this savage orange crop on a female person who had formerly been so pale pretty pink in public. The hair was vital to the creation of her mystique. One tale to surface at the time claims that the crop went public by mistake when a punter reached out and removed its owner's long dark wig during an early Eurythmics show at Heaven, the famous gay disco in Charing Cross. Ms Lennox

The Look that launched the Lennox phenomenon. Now a mass-market Grafika postcard.

has since said that the incident took place somewhere else. But Heaven – the European Boystown Mecca most nights of the week – fits better in this myth.

Annie's haircut made a big contribution to the vogue for gender confusion. Most participants were men who looked like women. Lennox was the reverse. Music culture has got used to sexual ambiguity in its male heroes. The campy, kitschy tradition goes right back to the beginning with Little Richard, and half the Presley controversy was bound up in his slicked-back, collar-length hair. So as Boy George, then Marilyn and later Pete Burns drag-queened their way to notoriety, it was almost conventional. They trod it more boldly, but the ground was still familiar.

Annie Lennox, though, was a rather different handful. For a mainstream society well used to the fey male, but pretty much untouched by women dressed as men, this bullet-headed beauty in a business suit spelled confusion; and the best example of it is the story of the video for *Love Is A Stranger*, the second Eurythmics hit.

The song is about passion objectified, being more entranced by your fantasy projection of another than any reality you might ultimately find. In the accompanying promo (directed by Mike Brady), Lennox plays the part of a high-class hooker riding in the back seat of a limo. Her partner, lurking behind his shades, plays the chauffeur. Suddenly, the singer whips off a bunch of Farrah-Fawcett curls and reveals – gasp! – the fearsome orange barnet.

On America's notorious 24-hour channel MTV they loved the new English pop people, and by late 1982 they'd built their reputation on them. All those luxury videos, manufactured precisely for the requirements of cathode tube! All those pretty young faces! For them too, it was almost Yesterday again, men in frocks or not.

But apparent women dressed as men were something else again, and when they saw the clip, MTV, a readily compromised institution within America's hideous return to 'wholesomeness', got themselves into a tizz. After all, look what the Moral Majority had done to TV shows like *Lou Grant* and *Soap*. They decided they would only put the video on air once a birth certificate had been sent over from England to prove that the singer really was a she and not an extremely earnest transvestite.

Here we had All American Paranoid Stupidity at the top of its form. The fact that the creation of illusion and doubt was the purpose of the entire operation seemed to elude them. So too did the fact that the production looked the same, birth certificate or not. But that was not the point. What was required was moral comfort. Boy George, whose very name defused his gender juggling even as it compounded it, they could handle as a highly personable gimmick – like Tiny Tim with talent. Annie Lennox, though, seemed to put all sorts on edge.

What is most peculiar about the fuss the Lennox Look stirred up is that Eurythmics were, above all, a most personable and reasonable pop unit. As public personas and as musicians they were pleasant and sophisticated rather than brashly subversive; grown-ups among the teeming newborns of contemporary Teen. The Lennox variation on androgyny chic was impeccable in its cleanliness, yet it was this little wave of controversy swept up by the crop and the donning of a suit which beamed her into the camera's eye.

The Eurythmic look was a narcissist's skit on uniformity. The initial idea of the suits was to promote a startling neutrality. 'Me and Dave like to think of ourselves as twins,' Lennox explained to Elissa Van Poznak, writing in *The Face* at the close of '84 (by which time she looked rather different); 'Quite some time before this gender bender business we both went to a very ordinary gent's tailor and had identical suits made. It made us feel like a unit . . . Americans caught on to it more than was anticipated.'

As an image and as a celebrated voice, this ambivalence – this sparkling non-commitment – is the key to the Lennox performance and hence the Eurythmics' celebrity impact. Juxtaposing a neutral, businessman's threads with a jarring, alluring head and facial impact (scarlet lips and a luxurious smile) Lennox became a glistening alien, an outsider in disguise. Detachment, then, was a glaze painted over the strains and stresses explored in the songs which took the duo to the top. Their visual impact was an equal partner to their music, not a prop – an irrelevant knee-jerk accusation so many old hat pundits have invoked when dealing with the 'new pop' break out. With Eurythmics, image was not a fig leaf, but a component in the conception of pop which was as important and creative as any other.

The *Sweet Dreams* album provides a classic example of the modern pop package at its most accomplished. We begin with the cover. Encased within a grainy, grey graphic surround is a small photograph of Lennox. Snapped from behind, her almost-nude form is effectively de-sexed, and further de-personalised by a black mask across the eyes and a matching pair of gloves. She offers loud red confection in a heart-shaped gift box. 'I believe you only experience love with strangers,' she once opined; 'you're usually just in love with the *idea* of somebody.'

The tracks on *Sweet Dreams* mirror the sleeve's careful geometry, with Stewart's synthetic music occasionally funked up by guest bass and horn players. The result is a cross between the conventions of Germanic machine disco circa '75 and the liquid cool of sweet American soul. On some tracks, melodies emerge with formal logic, while *Jennifer* – in which Lennox appears to be serenading a woman resembling herself – and *This City Never Sleeps* are mechanical mood pieces. In this, the first Eurythmics sound to find commercial favour, Lennox's voice half apes the music's stainless precision, half colours in the spaces it leaves.

The album's lyrics similarly oppose abrasive emotions and submissive ones. Love fights it out with loathing. Self-possession is mixed and matched with listlessness. The songs are organised with an absolute sense of order, but seeping through each framework is a sense of spiritual isolation and unease. *Somebody Told Me* is nightmarish. Their version of Isaac Hayes and David Porter's *Wrap It Up* at first seems too upfront alongside Lennox and Stewart's more demure compositions, but ultimately it is in perfect sympathy with their fascination for love as a commodity. In Eurythmics' world, it seemed back then, every nice thing was tainted in turn by its equal and opposite.

With sound, vision and mystique all tied up together and beautifully wrapped, Eurythmics were the perfect gift, and throughout 1983 they carved out a huge media space for themselves. Even behind the scenes they were a model of how recessionary pop operations work. Sobered by past experiences in conventional bands, and aware of the scope for versatility and self-containment offered by electronic instruments, they re-invented themselves as a compact creative unit in the contemporary mould.

A legend took root. Lennox and Stewart had known each other well for some time, and were a little older than their Top Forty peers; both were past their middle twenties when Eurythmics was formed. They'd originally met when Stewart and a friend called Pete Coombs were looking for a female singer. Annie, then working as a waitress, was, he said, the *healthiest* person Dave had ever seen. She was quite the opposite of him, a flagrant acid head with experience in every kind of band imaginable; 'progressive' rock, electric folk, experimental, punk. Stewart hailed from Sunderland. Lennox had been educated at a High School for girls in Aberdeen and was classically trained in the flute. The odd couple became lovers, and, as part of garish power-poppers the Tourists, had a couple of hits, the best known being a cover of *I Only Want To Be With You*, a success in the '60s for Dusty Springfield.

The Tourists dissolved in tears and gigantic debt. The group's dodgy legacy left Lennox and Stewart with a credibility problem. They had decided, together, to obliterate their pasts, and become self-managed, self-produced, self-sufficient and self-directed. The story of their lives together before and since that decision, especially in view of the recurrent subjects of their work, is now part of their mythical resonance.

Their new name was, on the obvious level, a hybrid of two words, 'European' and 'rhythmic'. It is also not a million miles away from the spelling of a mind and body discipline – 'eur*h*ythmics' – which became popular in the middle of the century, and is often cited as a precursor to the '80s rage, aerobics. With new handle in tow, the pair recorded an album in Cologne with noted producer Conny Plank, Blondie drummer Clem Burke, Holger Czukay and Jaki Leibezeit of Can, DAF's Robert Görl, and the son of Karlheinz Stockhausen. The resultant eclectic selection of experiments, *The Garden*, didn't sell, but enabled relations to be maintained with RCA Records. The legend resumes: Stewart became ill, Lennox had a breakdown, and the love affair ceased. They decided to stay friends and keep Eurythmics alive. With an advance from RCA they set up a simple eight-track studio in Crouch End where they recorded what would eventually become the *Sweet Dreams* album. It came out in the UK at the start of 1983, and, almost exactly one year later, Annie Lennox was sharing the cover of *Newsweek* with Boy George. The cover line: 'Britain Rocks America – Again.'

It was a caption which, with hindsight, seems like an omen, but at the time Britain wasn't 'rocking' America at all. It was *wooing* it with pretty colours and shiny shapes, opening up a neglected market space which the appalling inertia of the US industry had failed to fill satisfactorily for years. It was putting music and pictures back into the hearts of the young, and, in the case of the more adult performers, intriguing the children of the Baby Boom. Lennox attracted extra attention as the only woman of the so-called 'British Invasion', and she couldn't be discounted as a novelty; she was too cool, too mature, too strong. And for all her distinctly radical tinges, more than anything she represented a picture of female assertiveness which America's Jane Fonda liberals could warm to in numbers as great as its new generation of youth. And in Britain we weren't far behind.

Lennox's gift, though, was that she could not be pigeon-holed in terms of pop culture's past, *or* its shimmering present. She has been glibly dubbed the white Grace Jones, but the woman who hit Russell Harty, a former queen of the gay disco underground, was a *man*-made phenomenon. She was sculpted in vision by the dismal Jean-Paul Goude, moulded in sound at Compass Point Studios, Nassau, and emerged as an electro-Amazonian object, a kind of predatory Afro sex android. It's not surprising that many found the whole affair to be in very poor taste.

Jones was a cartoon. Lennox offered many more dimensions, crafted by herself. She shares only Jones' robotic body metaphors, but with Lennox, this was not an end in itself, but a device for conducting a dialogue, and on the next Eurythmics album, *Touch*, the *Sweet Dreams* photo symbolism was inflated to take up the entire sleeve. Clad as before, the singer poses for Peter Ashworth's camera, offering a warped flexing of a bicep. Her mouth is set hard. Her blue-green eyes – a harsh contrast with the orange hair – glower from their black surround. *Touch*: we might want to, but do we dare? This strictly contained body imagery is echoed in most of the definitive Eurythmics music. There's an insular quality about it that *sounds* like a slow-motion work-out. Lennox is frequently very soulful – Eurythmics records, like Culture Club's, were often played unwittingly on black radio stations in the States; a testimonial to America's enduring cultural apartheid – but the passion is portrayed as having been *learned* as much as directly felt. That's Lennox's talent, not her failure. On the early Eurythmics pop efforts she sounds like she's testifying, weightless, from inside a cut glass case.

Lennox's persona has been welcomed by many as positive and feminist, yet she is perhaps also a tribute to the rise and rise of the cult of the individual. Built into her self-sufficiency was a sense of isolation. It was a combination which made her more vividly contemporary than any of her women peers. She is a more complex creature than, say, Alison 'Alf' Moyet, now a 'quality' cross-over singer, but the female voice half of synth-and-singer duo Yazoo when Eurythmics burst into view. As Yazoo's first hit *Only You* came only a few months prior to Lennox and Stewart's breakthrough, comparisons were thick on the ground. Yet the two pairs could hardly have been more dissimilar. With Yazoo, the thing was de-mystification. Composer and synthesist Vince Clarke's whole attitude is the epitome of it. His jingles, tunes and arrangements with Moyet were so simple as to be almost flippant. To him, electronics are nothing *significant*. They're just a tool, a toy. Moyet's contribution to the whole came from what is conventionally thought to be the opposite pole to Clarke's silicon purity. Her voice and vocal style have always been in the traditional tough, bluesy tradition . . . *earthy*. The easy realisation of Yazoo's unusual combination helped take the pomp out of new musical technology, enabling it to mix the chip with Alf's altogether more elemental shout.

Lashings of self parody here from mistress and submissive servant alike in this RCA still.

Yazoo resolved contradictions. Eurythmics acted them out. The video for *Here Comes The Rain Again*, one of their more engulfing singles, is a good example. Set on a windy seaside cliff top, Lennox mouths the song, decked out like a forlorn Brontë heroine, while Stewart is seen following her around with a video camera. A video of the making of a video of a pop singer acting. Medium upon medium upon medium upon performance. It's a stunt which is too '80s to be true, and has become a video convention.

Here Comes The Rain Again emphasised the castaway aspect of Lennox more melodramatically than any previous Eurythmics song. But she continues to be hailed as a fresh form of liberated female icon. Ms Moyet, a statuesque, sometimes nervous woman, is directly inspired by the illustrious 'victim' tradition which goes back to Billie Holiday and beyond. Culture Club's impressive Helen Terry converted the same stylistic heritage into a camper brand of Big Girl Chic. Lennox though fused the new and the old to occupy territory only recently accepted in liberation circles.

Previous golden rules about not dressing up, making up, or defining yourself as a body (as opposed to a mind) have been broken in direct correlation to the 'counter culture's simpering demise. Sexual 'deviants' now join everyone else in the stampede for the mainstream. Defining yourself as a social leper doesn't get you places any more. Hence, 'gender benders', self-publicist neurotics like Morrissey of the Smiths, pretty, pouting sleazoid innocents like Marc Almond once of Soft Cell, or boldly politicised gays like the original Bronski Beat. The modern pursuit of 'style' (off-the-peg fulfilment through leisure; *The Face* magazine) and debates about *Desire* (a book edited by Rosalind Coward, a stunning, controversial Neville Brody cover for *City Limits*) have cut across old laws of logic. Suddenly, progressive people decided it was all right to be seen to care about clothes. You dressed *up*, not down, to express your dissent. Glamour could be subversive after all.

Thus, Eurythmics have a broad and loyal constituency among transatlantic yuppies. Annie is also a lesbian as well as a gay heroine, despite the S&M innuendo, since these are either seen as symbolic or feature Mr Stewart seated obediently at his mistress' feet. And for fading red grown-ups, in short, Annie Lennox is the missing link between Joni Mitchell and The Future.

In the standard fashion of history, the rise of Eurythmics' empire contained the seeds of its decline; and the story of the group since their emphatic scaling of the peaks of fame has been one of reversion to their many influences, rather than the continued squeezing of new combinations from the fruits of the past.

With the *Touch* album released, triumphantly, at the close of 1983, the threads of their tapestry were unravelled a fraction more. There is greater variation, warmth and confidence than on *Sweet Dreams*, and the first side remains crucial listening for anyone seeking the pulse of pop during the period. *Here Comes The Rain Again* opens the proceedings, then *Regrets* goes all mean on you; a funky, slinky, infatuation anthem. Next, *Right By Your Side* is a complete departure. Their first unrepentantly happy track, it was released as a 45 in an effort to undermine any moody blue metallic stereotype before it was able to settle; a mock-calypso celebration, it succeeded in its purpose.

But it was the side's closing number which most vividly illustrated both the source of Eurythmics' power, and the potentially debilitating privileges which that power affords entertainers. *Who's That Girl?* was a song of sheer self-reference, a clever example of a tendency which recurs across the entire pop field, manifesting itself as mock-corporate logos, as thematic symbols linking consecutive pieces of product, as video flashbacks to previous videos, or as musical signatures and lyrics referring to other songs.

Eurythmics, of course, indulged the temptation with the best possible taste, and, tellingly, the real trick was in the promotion, not the actual song. At face value the track can be accepted simply as a jealous girl's gripe with a sulky '60s feel. (An unusual scenario, for Lennox. Third parties like 'other girls' generally spoil the electric claustrophobia.) But the song's presentation as a single played exclusively on her reputation as the mistress of role-playing and disguise. On the picture sleeve an in-joke which only a true celebrity could get away with is perpetuated as Lennox appears unrecognisable next to Stewart as a greasy-looking spiv. The video re-emphasised the ploy. Set in a Soho-like nightclub, the clip features Lennox, '60s-style, perched on a stool, peering from behind a severe fair fringe. Stewart walks in with Meryl Streep on his arm. The *real* Meryl Streep, we ask ourselves? Sundry pop faces in various states of drag play bit parts, including Marilyn, before he'd been 'discovered'. (He would later become Annie's only rival in terms of genuine ambi-sexual beauty.)

What we had here was talent rejoicing in the comfort of recognition, shortly before wondering quite where to go next. The second half of *Touch* is oddly unmemorable compared to the tingling first, as the duo explore escape routes further from their former winning formula; and they have failed to discover a convincing one since, as 1985's disappointing *Be Yourself Tonight* album showed.

Aside from the deliberately blousey and attractively eccentric *Angel*, it was a collection which leaned heavily on structures and guitar attacks rooted firmly in the generally gruesome rock styles of the early '70s – the twosome's formative years. Eurythmics' detractors had always liked to claim that the pair were reconstructed hippies at heart, and, if that was unfair, then it was harder to defend them now.

Be Yourself Tonight is an album in sympathy with the terrible return of the riff, an outmoded rock method of little relevance to modern times. Rock's revenge has impinged most distressingly on the world of soul, to which Lennox's singing style owes so much. What a tragedy that her right-on duet rant with the great Aretha Franklin, *Sisters Are Doin' It For Themselves*, should epitomise everything club-footed and lumpen about soul's latter-day liaison with the piledriver rock-out.

The three bona fide Eurythmics albums have, alas, leaned progressively more on extra musicians rather than innovation, and when the tour to promote *Touch* featured a full conventional rock ensemble, it was a sad sign of things to come. At times it would be hard to distinguish today's Eurythmic muse from pure Adult Oriented Rock conformism, were it not for prior knowledge. It's not that the synth-pop blueprint offered inexhaustible options – far from it. It's just that there's a huge gap between Dick Cuthell's perfect trumpet embellishments on *Regrets* and the blunt instrumental thunderings and flabby ornamentation which has characterised so much that Eurythmics have done since.

It is perhaps a sad reflection on the inability of pop's public people to renew themselves that the most diverting Eurythmics music since *Touch* has been the sonic mood meanderings and Big Brother disco which comprised their soundtrack for the Mike Radford movie *1984* – an entirely different context, imposed by powers other than themselves.

Lennox and Stewart were among the cleverest participants in the revised game of pop. They plundered only in the interests of progress, they contrived a pop art approach that seemed rich in potential for deviation and growth. But this is the age of the short-life cliché, and, by their very essence, the most flawlessly formed are the swiftest to fall.

As a self-made product supreme, Annie is a true '80s icon, stuck rigid to her role in the spotlight. Perhaps the public Annie is doomed never to die . . . just slowly fade away.

4

MADNESS
Melancholics Anonymous

By the middle of 1982, Madness had turned into something fantastic, and they've hardly stopped being so since. Their string of hit singles had reached double figures. From rowdy beginnings as cartoon cropheads, the London branch of Jerry Dammers' Coventry-based 2-Tone label, they had devised a sound and a pop craft that was engaging, intuitive, incisively funny and uniquely their own. And to a hybrid music which drew on virtually every disreputable down-beat impulse of the previous thirty years, they added personality appeal. Everyone knew Madness. They were *local*.

The first three years of Madness trace the transformation of seven ugly ducklings into sober swans of wisdom and grace. Harsh experience helped hone them into magnificent survivors of a species under threat. The earliest Madness records are littered with their then recent memories of indiscrete boyish fascinations. They were boisterous, sometimes too much so. Within the infectious, laddish malarky of their early gigs and recordings, lurked an uneasy edge of menace which would be taken up, twisted and turned against them, threatening to cut them dead.

The earliest Madness records capture exactly the pros and cons of their perspective on the world about them. *One Step Beyond*, their debut album (for Stiff, who'd quickly snapped them up) comprised bits of silliness, celebrations of petty malignance and moments of picaresque delight in just about balanced amounts. They had this fascination with what's usually called 'lowlife'. Later they would sardonically observe it, but at first they liked to line up alongside it. With *In the Middle Of The Night* they invoked the seedy proclivities of an underwear thief. *Land of Hope And Glory* an instrumental romp, came littered with the sounds and shouts of prison life. Other tracks proffered football terrace taunts and chants, and occasional marks of adolescent meanness. Their basic comic yobbery was tainted by a ripple of unease.

Madness say they wanted to be the people's band. In practice, they attracted a mainly men-only society of followers, and a neanderthal element within it threatened to ruin everything. As affiliates of 2-Tone, Madness were more than a group, they were part of a craze, with a uniform, rules and a Past. 2-Tone's and Madness's inspiration – ska and bluebeat from Jamaica – had been popularised in

Left to right: Bedford, Woodgate, Foreman, McPherson, Barson, Smyth, Thompson.
Featuring: number one Regulation crop, Campari 'casual' or Harrington Jackets,
Levi jeans, Doctor Marten's boots. Madness crash into Wall Street, courtesy of Jill Furmanovsky.

Britain by skinheads at the tail end of the '60s and the early part of the following decade. As such, it had become the appropriated soundtrack of what turned out to be a stubbornly conservative youth cult of the white working class. 2-Tone brought the Crombie overcoat and Air Wair sole back out of the closet. But with them came the National Front and the British Movement, twin splinters of a fragmenting fascist hardcore, still seeking to feed off the deepening gloom of recession. A number of shows were wrecked.

The existence of a pro-Nazi following seemed to leave the group bemused. They were pressured, rightly, by many in the rock press who'd spoken out consistently against the thug Right's incursions into Punk, to disown the Swastika fan club.

Madness flailed about. It was the *illogic* of it which appeared to defeat them. Reality clearly contradicted ideology. Madness looked around and saw that white wearers of Union Jack badges sometimes had black mates. Ska was black music. *The Prince*, the first Madness single, had been their tribute to legendary ska-master Prince Buster, a Jamaican folk hero. The rocksteady beat they sang of would spawn reggae as its descendant, a mouthpiece for black identity as the decade wore on. Every other 2-Tone band – Dammers' excellent Specials, the Selecter, the Beat – had prominent black members in their line-ups.

Inconsistencies were everywhere. But then rationality was hardly their tormentors' strong suit. 'Suddenly we were getting pulled into something we didn't want,' Carl Smyth, chief instigator of Madness's Nutty Boy image would recall; 'we had this sort of non-involvement stance, but that meant things were getting misunderstood.'

For better or for worse, Madness foresook clear political denunciations. But theirs was a first-hand experience of a pervasive, desperate aimlessness which few others in the fey pop game know the first thing about. As bemused but bright observers of their own unnerving predicament, they must have learned a thing or two about the mad, sad badness in the world. And if their later work gives any clue, they didn't let it go to waste.

Madness understand so well about melancholia and comedy and where the two things meet. Beneath the gags and slapstick stunts that turned them into family favourites even as the furore faded, there has always been the taste of bitter-sweetness. And as the pop mart succumbed to the postures of designer rebellion, Madness took a glimpse of the past, a gulp of the present, comic cuts, and the tears of clowns, and put them on TV.

Pop success today demands an idiot box identity, and Madness remain peerless masters of the craft. The video boom gave them the chance to harness their comic gift to the demands of mass entertainment. Love songs or mad instrumentals, they made them all into video vaudeville.

Their first promos, directed by enthusiastic Stiff label boss Dave Robinson, were simple productions in which the group goofed about 'live' on stage, with the odd cut to dance-step interludes from sundry supporters and Smyth's alter ego, Chas Smash. But with *Night Boat To Cairo*, they got first scent of a video groove that made them supreme. The spoof Egyptian adventurers' tune was inflated into three and a half minutes of abject lunacy in pith helmets and khaki shorts; a performance of perfect pantomime. For the blossoming number of TV shows with a pop component, material like this was heaven sent. Madness became knockabout personalities. They grabbed the public by the funny bone and squeezed it till it hurt.

Where others treated the new visual medium with a reverence which could only be the patron of pretence, Madness's videos were one laugh after the next. But comedy, as all the best humorists know, is a serious business. And, in their growing gravity, it became clear that Madness were going against the grain. As a fresh breed of media darlings existed to be gazed upon, this was a group which preferred to do the gazing, and as their musical and compositional sophistication increased, so they developed a matchless knack for picaresque portrayal.

Bed And Breakfast Man and *My Girl* were just fledgling examples of what grew into a string of brilliantly economical pop narratives. Both were written by Mike Barson, keyboard player and the man whose piano the septet would gather around at recording sessions until he left the group in 1984. Barson's oblique contributions on piano and organ filled the fabric of the Madness noise with the archaic, lunatic, sometimes sinister flavour of music hall, silent movies and fairgrounds; timeless signatures of dusty yesterdays that the country seems too tired, sentimental or just plain afraid to ever sweep away.

Barson's bits, Lee Thompson's parodic saxophone and the irrevocably off-the-wall rhythmic sense of Chris Foreman (guitar), Mark Bedford (bass) and Woody Woodgate (drums) were the sum of a sound undiluted by the strengthening swing to transatlantic uniformity. In Smyth/Smash they had a ringmaster, and in Graham McPherson – Suggs for short – a singer of moderate range who more than compensated with a deftness of touch which brought words to life, and a neat, off-beat manner before the camera.

What we had here was the illusion of a golden-hearted gang of lads picked straight off the pavement, and Madness tickled The People pink by asking them along as well. Their video for *Return Of The Los Palmas 7* featured passing patrons of a Camden Town cafe helping them in their cha-cha send-up of dinner suit society. Newsreel flashbacks whirl by in random snatches; post-war history's greatest hits.

As their feeling for their own roots and context grew, so they transcended the cult that made their name, and achieved an ironic perspective on their lives and times which was – and remains – chronically absent from most popular culture of the day. *Baggy Trousers* (from their second album *Absolutely*: 1980) was their first hit to wave goodbye to skinhead/suedehead looks and manners. 'It was definitely nostalgia,' Smash/Smyth would remember of their desire to revive their own teen age; 'the nearest I ever got to that style was, like, a pair of boots and a pair of brogues. My dad wouldn't let me get my hair cut. My cousin did though. He was a big hero at the time.'

Baggy Trousers' lyric comprised McPherson's litany of playground memoirs. In the video, the group perform outside a modern classroom block, grubby gangs of 12-year-olds play football in the park, while, from nearby tower block balconies, bored housewives look on. Lee Thompson appears suspended in mid-air in a pair of tent-like strides of the sort the song describes, and a red stick-on nose. Madness were the clown princes of comprehensive humour. The world was their circus, but the London Borough of Camden was their home.

As Today becomes more futile, people want it to be Yesterday. But for the TV generation, yesterday comes not from a grandparent's memory, but in a moving picture show; from movie re-runs to rose-tinted wartime memories. Madness's talent has been to re-connect the TV image to the stuff of daily living. By refusing to treat the tube as anything but a tool for entertainment, their impact ends up being that much more profound. TV likes to unplug the viewer from the world outside. As true TV maestros with a sense of the past, Madness help put the plug back into today.

In their small-screen personas, as well as on disc, the group helped in the resuscitation of an archetype long associated with a national spirit up against the wall; the cockney wide-boy charmer. Punk era rock and pop had already hailed his return in the form of Ian Dury, Jimmy Pursey, Squeeze and more. Since then we've had George Cole as Arthur Daley in Leon Griffiths' brilliant *Minder*, Smiley Culture, Lenny Henry's Delbert Wilkins. . .recessionary pop offers a spiv variation for all occasions, and Madness were a brand new Crazy Gang. They used every new pop medium to create electronic music hall in your own front room. Video was invented to advertise the artist. Madness used it to introduce themselves as the Star Turns down your street.

Madness perform rather than posture before the video's eye. Instead of offering pop songs drowning in a sea of promotion they create complete pop *routines*. For the outstanding 45s *Shut Up, House of Fun*, and *It Must Be Love*, we got just about everything: pathos, satire, tunes, storylines, jokes, dancesteps, funny faces and a moral to every tale. Their treatment of the last of these, originally a hit for Labi Siffre, illustrates beautifully their gift for timing, implication and warm but mordant wit. Siffre's version mixed high-density sentiment with guileless sincerity; exceptionally pretty, but not very deep. Madness set the tune to a dramatic crunch of guitars and horns, contrasted with the crisp formality of plucked violin strings and a reggae reading of each verse. The arrangement is itself a postage stamp epic. The video suggests a whole different set of associations. The basic theme is funereal. Members of the group are filmed from inside an open grave, sprinting, top hatted, playing underwater guitar to a killer whale, improvising a sort of surrealist mime routine dressed in black in a studio painted white. Love and death; you only know you'll miss them when they've gone.

Similarly double-edged is *Shut Up*. In pictures, the song is portrayed in the style of the Keystone Cops. Ostensibly it concerns the business of passing information to the police. But an underlying wistfulness casts a shadow across its literal meaning. Denial and betrayal; a passing of the buck.

These fascinations for mixing and matching the bizarre, the futile and the downbeat would later threaten to entrap and marginalize the group as the pop universe around them increasingly embraced flippancy as an article of faith. But on their 1981 album *Seven* they clinched, sweetly, everything their earlier efforts had promised. They were as eclectic as they were confident as they were accomplished. Unlikely visitors to the super-chic Compass Point Studios, the group (with their regular producers Clive Langer and Alan Winstanley) added a lightness and cleanness of texture to a newly fluid sound.

The cover of *Absolutely* had shown the band in crops and Crombies loitering in front of Chalk Farm underground. For *Seven* they struck a joke showbiz group pose wearing roomy suits of grey. It's a shade which also dominates the grooves, and in these songs, more than any of their other collections, they recall the dowdy sardonicism of the Kinks, or the deadpan middle years of the Beatles. *Seven* offered social commentary tempered with slapstick. Madness explored the dark, doomed laughter of those points in the cityscape where bowler hat society meets baked beans on toast.

Seven is a triumphant album. But even as you relished its glowing execution and captivating leg pulls, you got the impression that, just maybe, they were themselves falling prey to the feelings of pointlessness they evoked in their songs. In *Mrs Hutchinson* they cheerily satirised the National Health Service. In *Cardiac Arrest* they poked fun at the stress-ridden City commuter. But *Grey Day* portrayed straight the gloom of urban drizzle, and behind the superficial bounce of *Sign Of The Times* they show no mercy. Lurid media interest in the fate of other folk betrays not really compassion, but a morbid, deathly delight.

Madness's melancholy is so effective because it is rarely indulged to the point of hysteria or rhetoric. Their intuition for depressed acceptance is the more refined for its concealment within jollity and japes. Unlike the people in the song, Madness have always preferred to look where others avert their eyes or numbly stare. But they had come to a point where the mechanics of success demanded that they start examining themselves.

The Catch 22 of the great pop dream is that an urge for recognition is what takes you to the top, but its achievement is what finishes you off. Self-consciousness constipates the spirit – and that's usually the end of that. Pop, even for the penny-wise artisans of post-Punk, is still basically a fast burn-out process, and the bigger the bang, the deeper the silence in its wake.

When Madness released the single *House of Fun,* it became their first and only number one, and also marked the end of their life as downbeat jesters. Their first hits collection *Complete Madness* – set the seal on it. Where could they go next? Those who've survived after the first flush of pop fame have usually done so either by retreating into specialist corners, resorting to self-parody or disintegrating into sludge: see Eno, Jagger and Cliff. For Madness, the consummate singles act, yet to score a miss, where else was there to go but 'serious'?

'I think *Rise and Fall* was probably meant to be our Sgt. Peppers,' McPherson would reflect in August 1985; 'it was our attempt to be like the great Bee-attles,' he added with a self-deprecating smirk.

Rise and Fall was an earnest, unavoidable attempt at 'progress'. In it, we find the former Nutty Boys sunk deep in a monochrome world, seemingly engaged in a search for some assessment of their own worth. Despite the presence of two more miraculous hit 45s (*Our House* and *Tomorrow's Just Another Day*), it is an ornate, dense and difficult album. The group are dug deep into territory that is domestic, desultory and almost desperate, mocking, with greater bitterness than before, the pervasive human philosophy of life-goes-on. Suicide and monotony take the foreground. Tensions simmer beneath the boredom, threatening to explode into breakdowns too mundane to cause much surprise. A mother sees her kids off with a kiss – what a shame it's going to be their last.

In their earlier anchored innocence, Madness had made a brilliant kind of guerilla theatre out of pop practices. *Rise and Fall* took everything which had been effortlessly implied before and made it literal. The sleeve art has each member costumed as a character from one of the album's songs. Inside the gatefold sleeve, we find them crammed onto a tiny stage before a ragged audience of three. On the outside, Laurie Lewis has photographed them up on Parliament Hill. In the background, the group's North London locale stretches away into an overcast distance.

With retrospect, all this can be imagined equally well as a statement of intent or a statement of entrapment. But what cannot be argued with is that the difficult period which *Rise and Fall* denoted the start of has since been survived and transcended with great aplomb; and Madness's output since then confirms them, in this writer's eyes at least, as the finest British pop group of modern times.

Two more LPs have followed, at two yearly intervals: *Keep Moving* (1983) and *Mad Not Mad* (1985). Their fates and their accomplishments just about say it all about Madness's talent, not only for writing songs, but for evading pop's primary tenet – an insistence on transience – whilst never deserting the audience or the outlook that has served them best – and, crucially, never insulting them either.

The time space covered by these two records has not been an easy one. *Keep Moving* was the last Madness collection to bear the Stiff label, and also the last to be made with Mike Barson who decided to depart soon after its completion. In what was widely reported to be a state of some dismay and doubt, the remaining six set about forming their own company, which took the name Zarjazz – an exclamation

Messrs GS McPherson and CJP Smyth absorb rooftop vistas of the London borough of Camden. By David Corio.

favoured by Judge Dredd, arch villain of the comic book *2,000 AD*. The home of such artists as Feargal Sharkey (briefly), former Scritti Politti drummer Tom Morley, and soul act Charm School, Zarjazz is also the new outlet for Madness's own releases, and *Mad Not Mad* stands as one of the finest and most eloquent pop LPs of the decade.

As pop's standards plummet to new depths of banality week by week, the continuing though diminished popularity of Madness is a tribute to their grasp of those things in people's lives which are timeless and inescapable. Their progress is that of a steady rejection of the most miserable and negative things to infatuate our times as mirrored by our pop. *Mad Not Mad* and *Keep Moving* stood for history not nostalgia; for living, not for 'leisure'; for life rather than 'lifestyle'; for inquiry over blind acceptance. They are works which seek to understand and express the world around us, not kick it into a ditch or hide it away in a presentation box.

Madness's flair is for expressing an ongoing state of confusion. Their politicking – be it as supporters of Greenpeace, Red Wedge and CND or in song – though it has become more overt, has never been permitted to turn their passion into diatribe, or tempt their tongues out of their cheeks. Always they have sought to grasp the spirit of the situation, to root out the sentiments at play. At times on *Keep Moving* their tack became almost too oblique, but the fluidity of their most recent music and their re-injection of wit has enabled them to shade in the big picture for which *Rise and Fall* was a slightly clumsy sketch.

So, as the '80s have given us pop as a cacophony of deteriorating artistic dignity, Madness have given us *One Better Day*, an aching lament for the down-at-heel occupants of Arlington House, Camden's hostel for down-and-outs; *The Sweetest Girl*, a dream of a version of the love song by Green; *Yesterday's Men*, a mocking tribute to the eternally tardy fulfilment of recent political promises; *Michael Caine*, a darkly comic sideways glance at the glamour associated with subterfuge; delight in every detail.

Despite having then had 19 hit singles in a row, Madness were not invited to contribute to Live Aid, essentially a tabloid occasion for all the other aspects of its worth. They had though promoted their own benefit single, co-ordinated by Jerry Dammers. It was a new rendition of an old Pioneers song called *Starvation* backed with a specially written piece of African-style pop, *Tam Tam Pour L'Ethiopie*.

The record went into the Gallup national singles chart at number 41, but received next to no radio support. Reports from those charged with plugging the song at Radio One suggested that the jolly daytime jocks were a bit bored with this Ethiopia thing. 'Too ethnic', one of them said, exhibiting perfectly the type of unctuous western arrogance that promoted hunger in Africa in the first place.

The story of post-Punk pop is one of artful pragmatism subsiding into showbiz sanctimony. Madness's music is a bulwark against the tide, a sanctuary where you can find perspective, humanity, humour – *intelligence* no less. Somehow, enshrined in their music and their words, there is a collective social memory closely approximating that of so many of those who've grown up through these last fifteen precarious years. Madness are the best pop entertainers because they reach beyond the boundaries of what we're told entertainment should be. People remember Madness because Madness remember them.

5

SPANDAU BALLET
Style Off The Peg

You need a *concept* these days, if you're going to get on. Ask Spandau Ballet. They wouldn't have got where they are today without one. Right from the start these youth-culture-obsessive Islington boys defined themselves as an *idea* as much as anything. They fed the outside world a manifesto, a collection of aspirations and principles. Not one single item of this manifesto has been welshed on. It's not often you can say that. Spandau have been as good as their Word, and the proof is there to behold. Why, even today you can see them swanning around north London in ravishing, rakish sports cars. On the back seat bottles of champagne – good stuff, mind, nothing cheap – nestle next to bags of frozen veg. Barely halfway through their twenties, these boys are millionaires. Porsche owners! Good old Spandau. They didn't let us down.

To invoke muso-puritanism at this juncture, would, as ever, be missing the point. But it is still instructive to note that in terms of actual *music* Spandau Ballet scarcely exist at all. Never have, poor loves. Consider their very first single *To Cut A Long Story Short*; flat, sub-elementary electronic thud-funk, it was of precious little use to anyone on its own terms. But that was not the issue. It was the *connotation* that mattered, and the single and the band were propelled towards chartland recognition on a groundswell of excited rumour. Spandau, it seemed, represented a whole new thing, a very special secret something, making ready to reveal itself to the outside world. It was this that got them their early heavy breathing headlines.

Similarly, *Parade*, the LP Spandau released in 1984, though a very different *sounding* thing, has broadly the same effect. As an aural experience it is just so *proficient* that you hardly notice it happening. Its primary function is as a soundtrack; showbusiness kids making movies of themselves; a backdrop to the doings of the vindictively young and rich.

Indeed, *Parade*, like its predecessor *True*, is a profoundly symbolic record. It is clinching evidence that the final clause of the manifesto has been fulfilled, specifically that Tony Hadley, Gary Kemp, his brother Martin, John Keeble and Steve Norman should be absolutely rolling in loot, and, crucially, *that it's nothing to be ashamed of*.

Now this is the crunch point, the key to the Concept. Because of it, reaction to the glorious lifestyle plan of Spandau Ballet has been ferociously mixed from the

Chrysalis promotional picture capturing exquisitely the cocksure latter-day Spandau leisure conception – as yet unavailable through the DHSS. Left to right: Kemp G, Hadley T, Keeble J, Kemp M and Norman S.

moment it began to spurt, perfectly formed, from gorgeous Gary's and manager Steve Dagger's mouths.

Controversy, as usual, shifts product. And even though by any sensible yardstick Spandau and their self-publicist ilk were about as controversial as Cliff Richard (and half as revolutionary) they so perturbed the established wisdom of rock pundits that controversy came to them. This was their greatest asset.

Broadly, Spandau proposed the unsullied desirability of dressing up and getting ahead. Their detractors tended to abide by the romantic tenet that true rock'n'roll was about dressing down, and dropping out. To this, Spandau ideology had the perfect counter punch and the opposition walked right on to it, jaw jutting foolishly and glassy eyed. Rock-think, rejoined the Spands, cherished a misty middle class vision of the culture of The Kids on The Street. The reality was, they pronounced, that the impulse of society's have-nots was not to express disenchantment through ass-kicking rock'n'roll, but simply to get on with improving their lot – by making up their own rules if necessary.

The logic of this was obvious: if you haven't got it, you want it (it's human nature, innit!?). The game was to make something special and unique of yourself. To look like something elite, even if your wallet said you weren't.

Spandau Ballet were not stupid. Nor, to a point, was their concept. People certainly seemed to go for it. Whispers from the underground led to them being the subject of a whole edition of the TV programme *20th Century Box*. Then, somewhat incongruously, they appeared on the cover of heavy rock-biased paper *Sounds*. Successful marketing requires the creation of saleable categories, and the handle 'New Romantic' became attached to them and their gaggle of friends. A 'movement' was born. *Long Story* made the top ten. Life would never be the same again.

Spandau Ballet were such a smooth, soft sell. The music business, the general media, the mass of pop consumers, all either fell at their feet or went for their throats. This was the cleverest thing about Spandau Ballet. They polarised people. An operation nurtured in its own self-consciousness – a self-consciousness which went beyond mere 'posing' – the only way they could really be hurt was by being ignored.

Even accusations of toying with Nazi chic simply doubled their column space. The appearance of their debut album threw critics into uproar. Entitled *Journeys To Glory* its pure white sleeve bore an embossed athletic Aryan torso design, the creation of one Graham Smith. Inside the gatefold, the purchaser came upon a burst of purple prose describing the 'soaring joy of immaculate rhythms', and 'the sublime glow of music for heroes.' *What* kind of 'movement' was this again?

No matter. If the clod-brained insensitivity of this sort of symbolism had passed the Spandau batallions by, the uproar they caused was easily turned to their favour. We live in hype society. Ignorance is fine, so long its profile is high, and if Spandau knew about nothing else, they knew all about pumping themselves up. The *NME*'s review of *Journeys* was quietly dismissive on the grounds that much loud talk concealed only moderate action. But *Melody Maker* and *Record Mirror* (now the excellent *RM*) went in hard. The sleeve note, signed 'R.Elms', prompted *MM* to quote in response *Tomorrow Belongs To Me*, the Hitler Youth song featured in the movie *Cabaret*. 'A little knowledge,' said *Record Mirror* with general reference to the package's imagery, 'is a dangerous thing.'

There has been no more apt summation of the Spandau Way. But the jibe was fuel to the fire. The following week, letters appeared in each of the papers, one each from the band and from R. Elms. 'We are all quite conversant with the political history of the 20th Century,' quoth the band, 'and we don't need lectures from you or anyone else. Yours is the ignorance in not realising that heroic and classical imagery has been used in many other contexts, too numerous to mention.' Miaaow! 'The idea of heroism and joy is of pride in oneself,' pronounced R.Elms, rashly revealing himself as the holder of a degree in History and Politics from the London School of Economics; 'working-class youth making the most of their own creativity, rejecting the stereotype that would have their class living in the gutter and loving every minute of it.' Further, R.Elms boasted of a 'lifelong involvement in working-class socialist politics.' So there!

Spandau Ballet: Street Art Socialism or Designer Tebbitism? The answer scarcely mattered, because Spandau Ballet were news, and they certainly knew how to talk. Songwriter Gary Kemp, 20, and Steve Dagger, 21, another LSE graduate, did most of it. Spandau introduced the music media to a world where the values rock culture nurtured in the privacy of its newsprint pages were utterly despised. It was their bid for a piece of self-made pop cultural history. 'The whole scene attracts people who want to develop, who want to achieve something, in any direction,' Kemp told *Sounds* correspondent Betty Page 'whether it's art or whether it's money. It's ambition.' In the rhetoric of Punk, to be called a 'poser' was the ultimate insult. But where Spandau came from, 'posing' was a way of life. 'The majority of people who come to see us are interested in two things: enjoying themselves, and looking good,' said Kemp.

Spandau portrayed themselves as musical representatives of a unique underground species. It involved 'a couple of hundred people, top wack.' It went on, not at grubby old rock venues, but in dance clubs which lurked, unnoticed by sloppily turned-out rock critics, in the basements of Soho and Covent Garden. A new lexicon of landmarks emerged: Billy's, St Moritz, Chaugaramas, and, most significantly, Blitz. To a soundtrack of soul, jazz-funk and, at the radical fringes, Euro-electronic dance music, 'creative' people – hairdressers, designers, general hedonists – admired each other and themselves. The coming-out of Spandau introduced the hick world at large to a new set of important priorities; presentation, mutual adulation, *style* – the catchword of the times.

Young people used to worry about pimples – now, they worry about *style*. It wasn't just a question of parading about in left-field threads. It was to do with how you defined yourself through every surface facet of your life. By extension of the principle, Spandau spokespersons inflated their leisure pursuits into myth. They turned magazine space into advertisements for themselves. R.Elms, reminiscing, in the short-lived London music weekly, *Trax*: 'Neitsche and Sartre cropped up most regularly when philosophy was on the agenda. Musical debate centred around Beethoven, Sinatra, Funkadelic . . . while Russian graphic design, German cinema lighting and north London football teams were all topics of lucid, if occasionally inebriated, conversation.' The Ballet and their boys proposed nothing less than a complete design for living.

When, in 1980, Chrysalis Records signed the group, they circulated a euphoric press release. It quoted the company's Joint Chairman of the time, Chris Wright: 'We are delighted to have signed a group which is undoubtably one of the most original and innovative to have emerged from the UK in the last few years. With the tremendous technological development that is about to take place in the record industry, and with greater emphasis being placed on visual creativity, Spandau Ballet are destined to become one of the major influential talents in the next few years.' To sum up, Spandau were: 'one of the most significant signings we have undertaken.'

It was clear that Chrysalis reckoned they'd got their hands on something more than just a group who might have some hits. Spandau Ballet were 'significant', the bearers of a youth ideology, a phenomenon to grab mainstream headlines; a little piece of the future, soon to become the present. In short, Mr Wright had bought the Concept, and he wouldn't be the last.

Spandau Ballet marked the changing balance between the conventional components of dissenting pop music's sales pitch. The hyperbole of every previous youth explosion had mixed adolescent self-obsession and neuroses with an edge of aggressive discontent. The beat and the look had included a sense of *threat*, some varying combination of guttersnipe violence and unbridled sex. Elvis Presley was the poor white southern boy who copied the black man's singing style, and infected young girls with lust. The Rolling Stones projected themselves as preening, perverted devil worshippers. The Who fanned the flames of the generation gap. The Beatles revelled in the false promise of egalitarian affluence. The Sex Pistols identified themselves with amorality and deepening social chaos. All of these reflected the simultaneous exhilaration and panic of runaway change.

But Spandau Ballet's was an introverted revolt into almost pure self-love. They advocated fulfilment, not through insubordination but through consumption. This was by no means a novel aspiration in the inherently consumerist culture of pop. But what was so salutory, so special and unique about the Spandau method was that they proposed this *as a moral virtue*; their public eye chit-chat *legitimised* the pursuit of the Good Life without humour, irony or passion. It wasn't that money and acclaim were what they wanted, but the fact that they afforded these inclinations intellectual credence. For Spandau, acquisitiveness was not just a way of life, it was a *philosophy* of life. *Journeys To Glory* – there's nothing coy about that.

Spandau Ballet *observed themselves* being different from the rest. Everything seemed to be done by logarithms rather than instinct. In part, this was because they couldn't play very well at first, and the svelte, sinuous dance music they first aspired to could only be achieved with musicianly technique. Their earliest noise – a clumping hybrid of funk and Euro-mechanic disco – was the nearest they could get. Topped off with Tony Hadley's 'heroic' operatic singing style, the result was as deliberate and mannered as the group wished to be hedonistic and ecstatic. More than anything, *Journeys To Glory* sounds awkward, inhibited and forced – programmed like a manufacturing process, in fact.

In this, Spandau epitomised an approach to what became voguishly (and appropriately) known as 'the pop process', which found great favour at the time. Other exponents included ABC, Scritti Politti (Rough Trade's bid to break out of the independent ghetto) and Dexy's Midnight Runners. What united them was that they were students of pop culture as much as practitioners of it. Entirely reconciled to the place of desirable packaging in pop history, they approached their art as an academic discipline as much as an emotional one – media studies as mass entertainment.

Of these, the least convincing were the Dexy's. Overlord (and, alas, arch bore) Kevin Rowland not only liked to theorise about 'soul' and 'passion', he made a great ham-fisted spectacle of himself attempting to deliver the genuine article. This was his mistake. Poor Kev just didn't have the natural talent to put his elaborate Plans into practice. ABC, Scritti and (while we're at it) the Human League were far more convincing because they rarely deviated from the stuff of abstraction. (When they did – ABC live on stage for instance – everything fell apart.) As such, they made designer pop records which worked both intellectually (music for critics by critics), and as polished, effective radio fodder. Words like advertising couplets, images ripped from everyone from Mills & Boon to Christian Dior, tunes pinched and customised from every page of disposability's scrapbook – it was pop as an in-joke, but it was lovingly conceived, and wore its tongue in its cheek.

The Ballet Boys model picket-duty chic appropriate for national dry-cleaning strike.

Like Dexy's though, Spandau were devoid of a sense of the ridiculous – especially in relation to themselves. Hence, their prefabricated sense of drama has remained unpricked by self-mockery, or humour of any kind. Everything pre-meditated (as opposed to everything sharp and vibrant) about their philosophy is set to their music, cut into their cloth, painted into their pictures. Their repertoire is infested with images of wealth which are devoid of self-parody or even a sense of mischief. As a result it is hard to see Spandau as anything but greedy pure and simple. There is no satirical tinge to the title of their second album. *Diamond* seems to get its name because its makers saw them glimmering in the middle distance. Later, there would be a grandiose epic called *Gold*, revived as an anthem for the '84 Olympics. Their look for the *True* album period pilfered the tweeds, cravats, paisleys and Brideshead haircuts of the landed rich without a ripple of a knowing smile. Steve Barron's *Lifeline* video immortalised a self-satisfaction which was glowing and apparently permanent.

Spandau's latter-day music simply oozes the blinkered confidence that affluence allows. Since the beginning their work has seized and exaggerated any symbol of magnificence, and never mind the context or implication. Spandau luxuriate in the facile grandeur that only a plentiful cash flow buys. In theory, if not in practice, theirs is no brash, vulgar celebration – it's *quality* and *status* they care about.

Thus, for the *True* album cover, they thought they'd have a bit of abstract art – you know, *art*. They got David Band to knock something up. The track *True* itself, their biggest international hit, was Gary Kemp's stab at something a bit classy; a ballad, something sophisticated like Sinatra or the Commodores. Dinner jacket stuff. Good taste. In August '83, Gary told *Record Mirror*'s Jim Reid about a bit of property he'd just bought: 'My flat's got character . . . if you take all the furniture out of it, it's got a style all its own. There's a lot of dark wood floors and shutters, and walls that have got a lot of dark wood on them . . . I like gadgets – good hifis, cordless telephones and stuff . . . I want to mix this with old style cupboards, chests of drawers, etcetera. Everything on remote.'

Everything on remote. That's Spandau Ballet all right. Even their emotions sound as if they've been conceived at drawing boards and discussed in seminars, or purchased off the peg. Camp followers have made much of their supposed depth of feeling, a kind of British municipal housing equivalent of the black American soul from which they have absorbed so much of their sound. But in practice Spandau express deep feelings with all the incandescent fervour of a shopping list. 'Soul' and 'passion' and 'pride' are invoked over and over, not least on *Parade* where 'pain' loses all trace of anguish to a self-congratulatory exchange of gold-plated grins, where 'passion' means a stylised toss of the fringe, and where proletarian pride comes across as glaring condescension: don't think, oh plain ones, that we've forgotten we were once like you.

With *Parade*, and the tour that tied in with its release, Spandau Ballet finally lost all touch with their original grand ideas. They've adventured into nothing but a jet set vacuum, with songs and videos about taming 'difficult' girls and being frozen in the frame of fashion. In their *Communication* video, they played at James Bond, a recurring theme among the most shallow of pop's new Designer Boys. John Conteh and Lesley Ash were roped in as extras; videos by stars, with stars, about being stars. Their hateful Wembley Arena concerts at the close of '84 amounted to a plain admission that they are now an operation better suited to giant mob-hutches than the refined surroundings of Sadler Wells theatre, or the Royal Albert Hall, both of which have played host to Spandau and their 'classical' longings. At Wembley, they exalted in their superiority, punching the air, grinding their backsides in the faces of squealing little girls in grotesque celebrations of power. So much for progress.

This, for the former 'Angel Boys', was an inglorious end to the trail. And what a tragedy it is, because in the beginning they really did have a point. They were right: reality no longer neatly conforms to those dog-eared romantic visions of the British working class fostered by the Labour movement (long-suffering, salt of the Earth) or north London's wholemeal cyclists (all that raw talent oppressed on 'the street'). But Spandau's antidote soon became just as redundant. It was all too much of a razzle, too purposeless a pose to turn any false logic upside down.

Spandau and other articulate faces to be embraced as 'new romantics' have been criticised in conventional quarters for denying reality and espousing escapism and fantasy. In the end it was tunnel vision sociology like this which enabled them to get away with so much guff. Spandau *did* represent reality, but only a part of it; an urban, acquisitive, pop media saturated working-class art-school reality which, for all its much touted pretensions to confounding daft bourgeois beliefs, became prime colour supplement material because its driving force is an urge to re-live a daydream of yesteryear.

The great media antidote to the ongoing ache of the '80s has been to seek out the shadow of the '60s. Not the '60s *per se*, but that Swinging, Carnaby Street 1960s where free-wheeling have-nots seized their moment and became moguls over night; where the white hot promise of progress was more than an idle product of Harold

Wilson's crafty imagination, because it seemed embodied in the laughing, joking, lovable Mop Tops whose fabulous elan the PM sucked up to on every possible occasion, those boys next door who ruled the world.

How the glossies loved the New Romance! How sweetly it fulfilled their urge to cram their pages with good news for a change. All the pretty '80s pages look the same. One week, Yoko Ono. The next, Steve Strange. This week David Bailey. The next, British fashion rules again. The Fake Swinging Sixties – fashion, faces, far out places, conspicuous consumption, so much more fun than the real thing had ever been. Spandau were right there in the foreground. The *Mail On Sunday's You* magazine even had R.Elms telling us that Blitz had been a bit like the Cavern; what better news could the readers wish to hear?

Spandau enthusiasts have drawn historical links with David Bowie and Bryan Ferry, clubland's first clever, soul-stirred conceptualists to be awarded intellectual clout. But the Ballet men have never sought to contrive stylised pastiche based on the cosmetic industries, or a nightmare of post-Apocalyptic savagery. Bowie and Ferry spoke for themselves, individuals commentating on their own predicaments; narcissism was a part of the act.

But in Spandau Land, narcissism was its own reward. As competent tunesmiths or (better still) as London boys who took the money and ran, Spandau would be acceptable – likeable even. But no, they had to be *valid*, they had to foist upon us an ideological heist. Even their annual gatherings of the faithful in Bournemouth had to be turned into press occasions, dignified as 'cultural events'.

Without the paraphernalia of 'significance', would Spandau Ballet have achieved the success they now enjoy? For years, an underground culture based on late nights, clothes, and sleek, sweet black American dance music had thrived, secretly, in London's West End, heavily patronised by suburbanites and out-of-towners making something out of nothing for all they were worth; struggling for a piece of the W1 action which said, 'I've arrived.' In recent times, the band Animal Nightlife have voiced that experience with more subtlety and warmth than any lifestyle sloganeer, largely because they've never *sold* themselves on the strength of it. Mixing soul and a cinematic elixir of '40s jazz, and fronted by Essex boys home product, the charming Andy Polaris, their *Native Boy* narrates beautifully the thrill of taking your place in the metropolitan footlights.

Spandau Ballet, though, wanted to be Youth Culture Leaders, and their self-promotion followed guidelines defined by youth cultural pundits. Their reading of the Meaning Of Mod – the cult of which they claimed to be descendants – was that of bush league sociologists. Thrift store nostalgia was all, as they heaved the myths of yesterday into the utterly different circumstances of today.

Delusion upon delusion. Those Swinging days when Britannia ruled the airwaves were finally just a force-fed illusion of classlessness, a sponge for fleeting popular wealth, and a tourist trap. As Spandau profess to re-live the broken Baby-Boom dream as icons of upward mobility, they fool everyone including themselves.

As theoreticians of youth culture they have defined themselves politically – as socialists. In '84 they stated their support for the miners' strike and, even as *Parade* hit the shops Gary Kemp could be heard on Radio One saying how he hoped his group's very existence was 'an inspiration to other working-class kids like us.' But, weekend Red Wedgies or not, Spandau's planning and plotting have only limited power to inspire. Their message, finally, is to achieve the scaling of heights which there's only room for a few to attain.

Thus, Spandau only goad their audience with their deeply conventional rise. They are, as stars are prone to being, untouchable objects of envy. They are guileless and stupid to pretend to be anything more.

6

DURAN DURAN
Doubt Free Adolescents

'Doubt' is not a word in the vocabulary of Duran Duran. For them, the purpose of life is simple. Though ostentatious and exotic, the boundaries of their universe are conservative and clearly marked. Though varied, their points of reference are conventional and easily defined. It seems that in their own minds there has never been the slightest question about the things Duran Duran should stand for or endeavour to achieve. And, like all successful commodities, those aims are enshrined and celebrated in their packaging.

The new stars of pop are united by their acceptance of the sales push. Faced with a choice between embracing the paraphernalia of promotion, or not, all have chosen the former with varying degrees of taste and grace. Duran Duran are most enthusiastically in favour. Indeed, so total has been their endorsement of the many new and novel ways in which a group can be transformed from a twinkle to a gleam in the public eye, that the line dividing the product and the ploys employed to shift it has all but disappeared.

Duran Duran have become associated so completely with the latest devices of commerce that these have ceased to be signposts or methods of persuasion. They are integral parts of the entertainment. They are a whole related range of things to peruse or purchase in themselves; just further desirable dimensions of delicious Duran Duran.

The result is that Duran Duran have become more than just a pop group expensively décored. They are a full grown tribute to the primary function of the advertising industry, that being to make nothing very much seem like something we must have. Look closely and you'll see that there is no tangible point of contact with Duran Duran – they are just layers and layers and layers of gift wrap.

When keyboard player Nick Rhodes and bassist John Taylor chose the name for the band they were set on building, they picked it because it didn't really mean anything. True, they stole it from a character in the tacky, spoofy erotic sci-fi movie *Barbarella*, a production whose essence they would shortly revive. But the appeal of 'Duran Duran' was that it was a blank page which they could colour in exactly as they wished. It was like a licence to make believe. It gave them unlimited options. And whatever Higher Purpose they may claim for their later work, what Duran Duran have done is point themselves with blithe, unconquerable zeal and certainty towards absolute fantasy. Just try taking that away from them.

Standard company studio shot for Is There Something I Should Know? *announcing final transition from mail-order extra terrestrial chic to jet set fantasia, with just a glimmer of sobriety. Left to right: Taylor J, Rhodes N, LeBon S, Taylor R, Taylor A.*

At the start, this absence of socially-oriented cant seemed a potentially fatal failing. In 1981, when the band first showed themselves to audiences outside the Birmingham club circuit, they rapidly became characterised as slightly witless purveyors of cardboard cut-out 'futurism', the desperate gamble of unfashionable EMI Records to make up for their comprehensive failures with Punk. Meanwhile, in the super-cool capital, Spandau Ballet, the first group to emerge from an overtly design-conscious London underground nightlife, had hoisted themselves into the realm of credibility with their loud talk of working-class upward mobility and radical self-expression through sound and 'style'. At the same time, a new breed of chart band – Haircut 100, Human League, Soft Cell, ABC, Depeche Mode – had about them an air of irony or absurdity or knowingness that Duran plainly lacked, while others in the vanguard of the new romance – Ultravox and Visage – bore the garish pomposity and self-regard of those believing themselves to be versed in the ways of Art. Duran Duran had few pretensions of this sort. There were no frills, no theoretical bric-a-brac attached to their impulse to be stars. In short, they seemed doomed. But with the doorway to the chart now wrenched well and truly open by pretty young men with flouncy hairdos and strangely tailored trousers, Rhodes and Taylor – now part of a quintet with Andy Taylor (no relation) on guitar, Roger Taylor (no relation) on drums, and a chubby, fringey singer called Simon LeBon – were able to move through it as well.

The scope of the 'new romance' had if anything been under-rated, and Duran Duran seemed to tap an emergent mass pop market of children and early teens weaned on *Star Wars* and video games. When their first single *Planet Earth*, emerged complete with synth, space-cadet wardrobe and lyrics like the script of *Close Encounters*, it proved perfect entertainment for the silicon chip-conscious white pubescent of the '80s.

Planet Earth bore many of the hallmarks of Duran's later, more vulgar triumphs. The tune is banal. Its lyric is almost as obtuse as the group's name was free from associations. As with the majority of LeBon's words, the effect is imagistic rather than specific. Close scrutiny suggests its theme to be that of making contact with extra-terrestrials. But 'close scrutiny' is hardly the point. The song works on a far more vague, associative level. The chorus sticks in the mind, as does the track's bubbling, cyclical semi-electronic beat, a slightly ham-fisted coupling of disco and rock. Put together with a checklist of trigger words and phrases broadly pertaining to television and angst – 'new romantic', 'TV', 'there's no sign of life', 'this is Planet Earth' – the appropriate ambience is created, the right *impression* made, and it was safe and familiar for all its eeriness. The record's overall effect is chromatic, passive, hypnotic; a series of signals conspiring in a drone.

A song tackling such cosmic subjects in so cosmetic a fashion from a group whose identity is implied rather than firmly defined is a dream date for a video director with florid ideas up his sleeve. Indefinite lines of meaning leave shiploads of scope for interpretation, and Russell Mulcahy had a taste for it.

A young man from Sydney, Australia, Mulcahy had made a name for himself in the medium early on, working with Trevor Horn's Buggles and with Ultravox on their bloated number one hit, *Vienna*. His production for *Planet Earth* now looks as dated as the band look embarrassed, but it still serves as a fine example of the ongoing Duran methodology and of the promo video's basic function. Created in shades of grey and blue, it comprises group and close-up individual shots of the band earnestly 'playing' interspersed with special effect segments where the singer is seen in thrilling proximity to the four basic elements of the Earth. The whole thing ends with Mr LeBon suspended in mid-leap towards a bottomless void; *Flash Gordon* without the laughs.

Thus, Mulcahy had competently executed each of the video's reasons for existing: to showcase the product, and to associate it with the maximum possible excitement. Furthermore, assisted by the fundamental blurriness of the popsters concerned, he was able to do more than just *illustrate*; he added a whole extra dimension to their dot-to-dot paranoia chic without destroying the fundamental impersonality with which the group sought to surround themselves. The music and the image formed the flexible framework. Video did the colouring in. The two inputs were in perfect sympathy.

In Duran Duran's subsequent rise to monstrous international success, Mulcahy's videos became more than just an important promotional adjunct. They were associated completely with the group's appeal. The videos advertised the group, who made the records, which were showcased through the videos. Mulcahy and Duran Duran closed the circle of creativity and commerce more completely than anyone.

With the 'futurist' fad petering out, the Taylors, Rhodes and LeBon found it easy to switch the focus of their fascinations. With Mulcahy at their service, they found themselves able to play the starring roles in making their dreams come true. And what *respectable* dreams they were. As teen adoration came their way, accompanied by the beckoning promise of gigantic wealth, they broke with their dilute sci-fi mini-dramas and propelled themselves into more tangible surroundings of adventure and affluence. But just because they'd got out of their spaceship, it didn't mean they'd come down to Earth. The serious business was only just about to start.

Duran Duran's *Rio* period is a milestone in the boom of video-pop. In America MTV was leaning heavily on promos imported from the UK to fill its schedules. This did much to facilitate the 'British Invasion' which was swiftly occupying a market vacuum created by the US rock industry's neurotic devotion to the children of the post-war population bubble, now well into its thirties and beyond. Combining, as they did, the appearance of something young and new with plenty of tried, tested and recognisable riffs, Duran Duran were tailor-made for TV-soused Stateside adolescents.

After a couple of slightly less satisfactory excursions with other video directors, the band re-united with Mulcahy for the *Rio* album's trailer single *My Own Way*. The group's management wrested a then unprecedented budget of around £30,000 from a reluctant EMI to go with a crew to Sri Lanka, the latest 'unspoiled' corner of the world to be colonised by non-package holiday-makers. There, they contrived the first foreign location pop videos.

It turned out to be the most cost-effective thirty grand the royal family of British record companies had ever spent. The Sri Lanka videos catapulted Duran Duran irrevocably from being the awkward appendages of a cult to being something entirely luscious and unique. The world became their scenery. Sri Lanka's geography and populace became props in an orgy of sub-cinematic self-gratification.

With the group's name now solidly insinuated into the public mind, Mulcahy was able to rev up to full power the methods and rapacious values of contemporary advertising. Alice-like, the band were able to pass through their own reflections into whatever rarefied role playlets they chose. In *Hungry Like The Wolf* LeBon becomes Steven Spielberg's all-American hero Indiana Jones, anglicised and suitably revised for the feverish pursuit of a savage 'tiger woman' who our man 'tames' in the jungle undergrowth. The clip for the accomplished ballad *Save A Prayer* presents a series of snapshot views of the island's sumptuous natural beauty and its citizens at work, as the leisured backdrop to a song about yearning for the perfect, bronzed, one night stand. You half expect a bi-lingual guide – or possibly Cliff Michelmore – to drop in and deliver the lowdown on local hotels during the instrumental break.

Duran Duran became highlife tourists. Only their souvenirs were ever likely to be ours. Symbiotically tied to their video representations. Duran's name came automatically to suggest travel, exotica, erotica, high-tech gadgetry and predatory passions, all just trotted out like the toys of playboys. Their fascinations were enticingly up-to-the-minute, state-of-the-art consumer crazes. They just threw together bits of everything that was all the rage: the born-again adventure movie; upmarket ad fantasies; new technology; high-class porn. Duran Duran transformed themselves into a leisure product that was a collage of other leisure products, and epitomised the desirability of owning leisure products; and all this crammed into three-minute bursts of dayglo entertainment.

It was artistry with a built-in sales pitch. Mulcahy's restless cutting technique fitted perfectly into the viewing habits and expectations of the public, especially in America. TV remote control units enable couch potatoes to not even *move* to switch channels. Anyone who's ever witnessed a would-be Californian penthouser in front of his wide-screen idiot box knows that concentration only lasts for tiny periods. The slightest demand for intellectual effort results in a change of channels. Zap! The zap is now an integral part of TV viewing. Duran Duran videos are like television with the zaps *built in*. You don't even have to press the magic button.

Escalating celebrity now allowed the group the luxury of self-parody. Further location shooting – this time in Antigua – produced more flashy promos with the one for the title track of the hugely successful *Rio* album being the classic Duran item. From aboard their holiday yacht, the boys take turns at impressing an elusive female beauty. The fun is in watching them fail amidst a cacophony of pink cocktails and champagne. Women, draped about the place, are periodically soaked in bubbles, ice cream and foam. Subtlety is hardly Mulcahy's long suit.

Apologists for *Rio* quite reasonably claim the video to be a joke at the group's own expense. But effective self-mockery presupposes an element of humility, and Duran Duran seem a little short of it. At first, what they exhibited was a routine and harmless kind of vanity; they just wanted to be boys on film. But acclaim seemed to transform this into the most loveless form of material lust. Everything that caught their magpie eyes had to be subordinated for their amusement. The message with Duran Duran is that human worth is defined *entirely* by what that person owns. Thus, we can't ever hope to be like them. We are fated to adore; all we can do is buy up their by-products.

The Durans have probably generated more saleable items than anyone but Michael Jackson. Indeed, Kasper DeGraaf and Malcolm Garrett have built their design and merchandising business, Assorted iMaGes, around them. An enterprising pair, they started off a magazine, *New Sounds, New Styles*, to record and explain the doings of the 'new romantic' folk, often with great insight and panache. They were the first to get the relative emphases of words and pictures right. Garrett, whose clever graphics distinguished the sleeves of all the Buzzcocks' records, was brought in to do the same for Duran Duran, and has stayed in favour ever since.

With Duran Duran, design is quintessential. Garrett's brief is straightforward. 'My job is to make it all look as if it's coming from them.' A chronological look through all the album and single sleeves shows how precisely he has translated the textures and fascinations of the music into shapes and symbols, then perpetuated them through time.

The Duran sound is clean, metallic, geometric, immaculately finished. So are Garrett's visuals. The sleeves for the first three singles and the debut album all abide by the same layout principles – linear precision, virginal backgrounds. Anonymous.

Then, June '81's eponymous LP gives us our first high profile picture, with the guys looking casually futuristic. Simon leans his loins against the bonnet of a big, mean motor car . . . that's more like it!

Rio picks up the thread, but changes the theme. For the album, flavour of the month American artist Patrick Nagel was commissioned to do a painting. Garrett placed the smiling, Asiatic features of the subject woman against a claret backing. Diagonal lines and tailback lettering give an impression of speed. A facsimile cigar label logo at the corner confirms the cosmopolitan theme. Apart from *My Own Way* (which preceded it), all three 45s lifted from the collection boast designs which recycle elements of the original: the lettering; the woman's eyes; a scaled-down version of the picture complete. That's product continuity, a parody of corporate identity, which nonetheless performs the same task as its inspiration.

The group's choice of Nagel was typical. They like to think they are in the vogue of good taste, they want to have the best. It has become part of their behind-the-scenes legend that they simply *insist* on having one, and only that particular one, brand of vodka to drink backstage. Nothing else will do. The best is the best is the best. It's all perfectly straightforward. 'I'm very happy with myself,' Simon LeBon told *The Face* in February '84: 'I don't think there's anything wrong with me.'

The rise and rise of Duran Duran ushered predictability back into an otherwise invigorating re-birth of conventional pop values. In reviving an old school reading of stardom, the new stars simultaneously poked fun at it. There was no attempt to cover up the essential trashiness of the showbiz business from clever chaps like Boy George. When the Boy winked at the public it was as if he was inviting us in on the joke. He created intimacy precisely by letting on that, between us and him, no such thing could ever exist. But when glory came to Duran Duran their response was fundamentally graceless. They abandoned any vestige of populism and finesse, and cultivated envy instead. Their idea of 'tongue in cheek' was to flaunt the privilege status bestows by making public wallies of themselves.

Inevitably, the media microscope began picking out the different individuals in the quintet. So Nick is clever and John is gorgeous and Andy is naughty and Roger is quiet and Simon is sexy and so on. Yet, for all the profiles and portraits they remain devoid of personality, just like the blueprint demanded. Think of Duran Duran and think of something blue, silver and flickering beyond your reach; think, in fact, of a sign saying 'keep off the grass'. It's all admiration and no identification. The documentary *Sing Blue Silver*, made during their '84 world tour and shown on British TV at the end of the year, features a scene with a security guard and three seriously overwrought girls. They plead with the guard to get them the band's autographs. The guard asks which names they particularly want. This throws the girls into a quandary; they don't *know* any of the names. They're here for the hysteria, that's all.

Duran's adventure holiday period lasted them comfortably through 1982. *Rio* provided them with a string of hit songs, a string of hit videos to match, and a successful Atlantic crossing. Their progress since then has been along the classic lines of the pleasure-obsessed rockpop phenomenon. Magicked into the isolating world of idolatry, they began manoeuvres to protect what they'd dreamed of accomplishing for so long.

Is There Something I Should Know? (March '83), their first release of new material for a year, marked a transition into a third career phase; a *neurotic* one. Despite the fresh sunlight intimation of Malcolm Garrett's artwork, and a photo for the 12-inch which showed the boys relaxed, tanned, and coolly clad, this was their most *hysterical* record yet. It's a begging song, solid bended knee stuff from shrieking, paranoid Sir Simon as the band crank out their nearest thing yet to sanitary, automatic rock'n'roll. The thing is littered with references to broken glass and running away and dancing demons at the door. It is also quite crassly sensationalist: enter the throwaway holocaust metaphor.

Russell Mulcahy's video also broke with the holiday sequence. It's a mainly studio-based clip with a geometric/militaristic look, spotted with flashed throwbacks to previous video works. This shift towards 'seriousness' and self-contemplation typifies a classic afterthought of immodest celebrity. It was time for the Duranies to start wondering what it was all worth. Their solution was to embark upon an apocalypse trip.

Looking back, Duran Duran's career comprises three big 'B's: Bowie, Bond and the Bomb. An insight into the latter can be found in the most useful of the numerous large-format softback books about the group, Garrett and DeGraaf's *The Book of Words*. Counter-balancing some rather routine knee-pad journalism is an interview with LeBon, conducted by DeGraaf around the time of the release of their single *The Wild Boys*: 'to me the song is a warning about the kind of world we could be heading for,' Simon explained, 'a world of total anarchy – and the kind of people that would be able to survive, and the kind of morals you can carry with you in that kind of world.'

Seven And The Ragged Tiger, the third Duran Duran album (November 1983), saw LeBon's recurrent lyrical phantasmagoria concentrated and darkened. The album's contents crawl with reptiles. The music was their most hostile yet. *New Moon On Monday*, *Union Of The Snake* and *The Reflex* – remixed for single release by Chic's Nile Rogers – all became hits, the last making number one when pundits were predicting the group to be a spent force. Reports suggest that extra care and attention went into the making of *Seven*. They really *thought* about it. 'I've always said that I don't want to mix politics with music, but you come to a point where you can't avoid it,' says LeBon in *The Book Of Words*; 'because the things that are important to you are political. When the whole civilisation is at stake, really at stake – am I am going to be around in the morning, or is somebody going to be stupid enough to press the button?'

All the Duran boys were very young when they space-hopped into the big league, so it isn't a crime that it showed. But even as LeBon's escape from puerility became reflected in his work, the most striking thing about his foray into 'issues' is that it still takes the form of dream imaginings. He remains a fee-paying sixth-form psycho-mystic at heart, an '80s edition of something that escaped from *If.* Maybe that's why his anxieties show little understanding of the powerful forces to blame for his sleepless nights. Maybe the main reason he wants to expose the beasties that crawl into his head is that they threaten his former sense of certainty. We get a display of distress rooted not in Planet Earth but up in Simon's private stratosphere.

Duran's explanation of this would probably sound like their justifications for early lapses into Very Poor Taste, like for instance the ghastly Godley and Creme video they commissioned for the distasteful *Girls On Film*; that is, they were only being 'honest'. As if any sentiment is all right as long as they weren't making it up. It's an outlook which certainly precludes daunting options like modifying yourself or confounding the expectations of your audience. 'We have always said, and still believe, that we are ordinary people acting purely on reflex in an extraordinary world,' writes LeBon in his introduction to *The Book Of Words* – a display of modesty to conceal a denial of obvious power.

Not until crackpot hysteria finally hit them and cocaine stories came screaming from the tabloids could anything of gravity cloud Duran Duran's comfortable minds. And it emerged – as it could only emerge – as yet more material for multi-

60

Simon the sensitive.

media glam horror fodder. Their fears of destruction are articulated through freeze-dried *Mad Maxisms* like those which dot the live *Arena* footage: rather grubby little voyeurist set-pieces with androids copulating, computer graphics which frame and home in on every stagey face that's pulled. Every emotion becomes just another hi-tech fetishisation of the stars themselves.

The problem with Duran Duran is not the mere fact that they are drawn to fantastical imagery, but the way they go about it. Everything is somehow cheapened into *Star Trek* with stardust. Pleasure becomes an almost vindictive pursuit, while world destruction is portrayed as a romance of tinsel and tunnels and tasteful lighting – a tawdry kind of substitute sex for kids who can't spell 'apocalypse' yet.

So, with the three-part drama of emulation, conquest and contemplation played out, what was there left? First, a reversion to stage two and the theme for a James Bond film, *A View To A Kill*. (Ironically it's among their sharpest music and also some of LeBon's most Ferry-like phrasing.) Next, holidays again, but this time real-life working ones, with half the group indulging themselves in The Power Station, the rest airing Simon's cast-offs in Arcadia. Are they doomed forever to be playboys in playbacks? Is there anywhere to go but sideways? Whatever, it won't bother these determined, self-made young men, because when all is said and done, 'doubt' is still not a word in the vocabulary of Duran Duran.

7

PAUL WELLER

The Growing Pains Of An Angry Young Man

Pop culture, arguably the ultimate capitalist liaison between idealism and hard-boiled cynicism, is, by virtue of this very combination, a reliable barometer of our times. So what does it say about today that there's nobody quite like Paul?

Truly, this Mr Weller from Woking is incredible. These days, you're supposed to take the money, be grateful, give a little bit away, then sit down and behave. So what does Paul do? He stands up and complains: 'I'm more idealistic now than I ever was,' he insisted, just after the end of the year of Orwell, a very big hero of his; 'I've been reading more, finding out more information, learning more history. Some of the people from history that have tried to change things have been more of an inspiration to me than anything else before.'

Coming from a self-made fixture of the pop aristocracy in this age of retrenchment, some of Paul Weller's declarations are almost unbelievable. He doesn't *care* if people say he's stupid. Somehow, he's just got more and more annoyed about the stupidity of everything else. Flawed and befuddled though he has sometimes been, no-one has so doggedly, so *trustingly* set their face against the prevailing wind of no change.

Contradictions, of course, abound. But the fantastic thing about Paul is that he refuses to be put off by these. He knows all about them, but carries on just the same: 'I'll have to make a dramatic statement . . . ' – bashfulness is brusquely brushed aside – 'I don't see why I can't do the same kind of agitational things in my music that authors have done in the past, or poets like Shelley. Alright, I know it's a crappy business I'm in. So you either surrender to that business and say "I'll just go along with it", or you *risk* that contradiction, stick with your ideals, and try to do something about it.'

Paul Weller is one of a species under threat. Like so many great grumbling public sceptics he is a Believer underneath. He cannot seriously accept that everything can be so dreadful, that humankind cannot be somehow persuaded to see the light and put things right. For all the bitterness he's been known to wear on his sleeve, Paul Weller comes across as a man with *faith* and he can't shake that off, just as he can't accept that music cannot be a motivating force in people's lives, rather than simply one that soothes or reflects. Paul wants his songs to wind the wrong people up. He wants them to egg the right people on. He's an evangelist in an agnostic world. Most pop exists to cultivate consumer gratification. Paul Weller wants something much more difficult than that – he wants consumer *action*.

Paul Weller's secret smile; by Peter Anderson

Weller was the only big name of Punk to survive its inglorious capitulation. With his massively popular band, the Jam, he entered the 1980s bearing a reputation based firmly in guttersnipe rock's rebel orator tradition. There had been some terse, tense, magnificently splenetic music crashed out on a drum kit, a bass and Paul's firebrand guitar; furious songs which started out frustrated, and turned progressively more sour, as Punk's burn-out rhetoric became the substance of a self-fulfilling prophecy.

The Jam though, simmered on. And in their longevity they proved that where the Sex Pistols had been a symbolic kamikaze outfit, and the Clash were, in many ways, deeply conservative, the Jam were diarists, historians. Though firmly of the present, they traced a line from the past which gave their work a rare dimension in pop – perspective across time – and as a consequence, a popularity which transcended fashion. The clichés are all true; the Jam *did* have a relationship with their audience which was as close to egalitarian as any fire and brimstone rock act and their flock are ever likely to get.

Unusually in rock, this comforting sense of mutual *permanence* did not have its bedrock in easy, reactionary habit. The Weller effect did not turn on transient shock tactics or guerilla art warfare, but nor did it function in a social vacuum. As such, it was able to prosper undiluted for an unusually long and useful time, and, when Weller finally did wrap the Jam operation up, it was not in the absence of options; his reading of the meaning of Punk encouraged him to use it as a springboard for a proud self-education, and a determined quest to maintain its declamatory impulse, come what may.

For Weller, the demise of Punk had not necessarily been inevitable. Rather, he saw it as a bunch of promises which were broken, or whose execution just went wrong. Style Council was formed, he says, not as a pragmatic career measure to cope with changing market demands, but as a better way of getting things right again.

Nonetheless, Style Council was a very different rack of trousers. As an organisation, it made a clear attempt to break out of rock's rigid and ritualistic mould. Council, meaning a gathering of people, ideas and (in this case) Politics. Style, meaning the extremely important business of projecting your soul through your wardrobe. It was an unwieldy title. But then it was the masthead of a project which would take upon itself a potentially unwieldy rôle.

Here was an entertainment unit which sought to function in a range of apparently conflicting spheres, partly in the hope of making them overlap. Style Council would involve themselves in the troubled ongoing relationship between supposed polarities like Politics and Pop, Reality and Romance. Weller, with his keyboard partner 'Merton' Mick Talbot and a handful of other, semi-permanent Councillors, has gone about his weighty task with an earnest deliberation and outspokenness which has thoroughly annoyed detractors both of his basic goals and his methods, and which has not always resulted in the greatest music. But what is most astounding of all, is the extent to which the Style Council have succeeded in their pursuit of the allegedly impossible.

If Weller is naive – and, often enough, he is – then let's have some more of it. If Weller is a dreamer, then at least his dreams are brave, bold, and big enough to be worth sharing. And if Weller is a self-indulgent romantic, then this must be the elixir of the very best pop if the first three Style Council singles were its upshot.

These were tracks, which, in their packaging and their grooves, still stand as handsome achievements in all of their intended respects. The debut, *Speak Like A Child* (1983) took a nimble bass line, a swirling Hammond organ, and a rush of melody, mixed them together and ended up a love song of fervent sentiment. The same year, *Money-Go-Round* was a furious, fuming, heckle of a thing, sheer, clattering, Anglo-funkoid agitprop – a political tract explaining war paranoia, social deprivation and contemporary faithlessness as symptoms of dominant capital accumulation. Then, in 1983's summer months, came a four-track extended player, *A Paris*, bearing a brace of breathless ballads, *Long Hot Summer* and *The Paris Match*.

Each of these 45s etched a different aspect of the Style Council's worldview, and, as a trilogy, they capture as well as we could wish the things that link them to their time, yet separate them from the crowd; their weaknesses and how those weaknesses are also the source of their strength.

In the first place there is Weller's deep fascination and affection for his country of birth. In the classic way of the royalist working class, he used to think that a vote for the Conservatives meant a vote for England and its glorious independence; how he heaped aggravation on himself in the earliest days of the Jam when he let this sin be known! Since then, of course, Weller's colours have changed from blue to resounding red, and his former nationalism to *inter*nationalism, as celebrated on the second Style Council album, 1985's *My Favourite Shop*. But where most British pop has acquired a mid-Atlantic sheen which can only be described by that overworked and sorely-abused adjective 'sanitised', Weller's work has retained a rich flavour of Blighty, even when his fancy has strayed to foreign lands. He is entranced by this country's neglected heritage, the one the tourists don't get to see; an England of class entanglements, civil strife, and radical writers, but most of all by those heady Harold Wilson years when England's youth seemed to claim the national identity for their own. It's the Swinging Sixties one more time: 'I suppose I was too romantic about it really when I was younger,' he reflects; 'but it seemed like such an exciting time to me. There were loads of things happening. There was young, working class people making it. The young kind of swept themselves up and made their own establishment that seemed quite separate.'

For the first phase of their career, the Style Councillors, and especially Paul, betrayed their ache for a bygone age of Carnaby Street in a manner which sometimes strayed close to a dewy-eyed revivalism. The photographer Peter Anderson was employed for a photo session in Paris, the elegant results of which defined and confirmed the Style Council look crisply and pervasively. There they were, all over the place: Paul Weller and his long white mack.

It wasn't a Humphrey Bogart, US private dick-type mack that Paul Weller wore. It was an English social realist mack, the sort of item anti-heroes wore in social realist movies starring Laurence Harvey or Albert Finney. It was there to keep the grey anglais drizzle at bay, but it was also Paul's tribute to a time he was too young to experience; a time when young southern sharps like him dressed better, danced better, and liked better music than anyone else in the world. They also had higher hopes. How those hopes have been dashed in the twenty years since; and how Paul Weller knows it.

It is in this clash between wistfulness and fundamentalist moral righteousness that we find the core of Style Council's occasional blunders, spasmodic brilliance, and above all their enduring populist appeal. If *Speak Like A Child* was a slice of exhuberant Blue Flames pastiche, and *Money-Go-Round* a blistering piece of playing for a harsher today, then the *A Paris* EP was a retreat into contemplation, and the art of mooching meaningfully. All three pieces of the Council puzzle were represented on their first LP, *Café Bleu*, released at the close of the year. The cover re-introduced us to the man and his mack, departing with moody magnificence from a Parisian café, and the cool allure of *le continent* et *le jazz* made itself known throughout much of the music inside. There were Booker T-ish instrumentals and slushy bits of balladry. There were some militant moments too, but one was in the form of a formal voice-and-solo-guitar ode to the downfall of capitalism. Weird! This might have been 'protest' but it sure wasn't PROTEST!

In fact, *Café Bleu* was a patchy, wide-eyed collection, too overt in its absorption of new influences to make something new of them. But what narked many of Weller's former cheerleaders in the music papers was its gesticulations, its fastidious blend of minutiae, its *quiet*. Where was the rage? Where was the fire? Where was the fulminating *thunder* of yore?

What some people failed to grasp was that *Café Bleu* was an attempt at a serious engagement not with sound and fury alone, but with those other aspects of the young '80s person's life which sadly fail to fall into a leftist theoretician's blueprint for the future; history, aspiration, survival, and finally relief. Paul Weller, in his obsessive, introverted way, was not struggling to create an identity which admitted both theory *and* practice. He wanted to mix revolution and the evidence of his eyes, to come up with his own ideal model of what the young, modern British working-class person could be.

The confusions of the new technology, the flailings of the British Labour party, and the general air of debilitated disinterest in anything outside of home entertainment have sparked off interesting media squabbles over the nature of the true English proletarian. The middle-class 'alternative' notion continues to endure, dreaming irrelevantly of all that sweating nobility just waiting to have its consciousness raised. Then there's the hip New Right reading, also known as the Spandau Ballet position, whereby all that everybody wants is two weeks in Teneriffe, a cash-in-hand domestic economy, and the chance to look the part you aren't. The truth lies somewhere else altogether. It is overwhelmingly smalltown and suburban (and, hence, perpetually ignored) and does its shopping in ordinary high street stores. It is a quiet, conventional creature, slightly bored, quietly desperate, and discouraged from doing anything about it from birth.

Youth cultural crazes have always overlooked the forgotten majority. They're not outrageous enough, they don't shift units, they are way down market and they're probably there to stay. Paul Weller's vision is to badger this corralled reality into believing that it *counts*. A suburbanite himself, he appreciates the space between the metropolitan and the small town experience. For an icon of an urban phenomenon, he sets himself vehemently against all the trappings which attend status of that kind. In this, he stands a mile apart from what most of his contemporaries are delighted to have become: 'Their attitude is that they'd like to go out with Princess Di or shag her sister or something. They wish *they* were aristocracy. They wish they had the aristocracy's sophistication, which doesn't interest me because I *hate* the fucking aristocracy.'

Weller's notion of sophistication is that it should signify dignity for all. New Romantic wanted to set itself apart, and Weller understands that need to make something special of yourself in the face of a world which says you're not. But at the same time he knows that rags-to-riches stars are not the vindication of free-enterprise. They are its willing hostages, the blunt instrument with which the mighty beat the rest of us into shamed submission. On the face of it, Weller wallows in nostalgia for those recent years when to rise up the social ladder was easier than at any time since the war, when upstarts of humble stock became the pet fad of the posh. But at the same time he knows the era thoroughly enough to see through its facade: 'It was all artists . . . photographers, fashion designers, musicians. But that's not the same people who are going underneath the ground and digging up coal or looking after the sick. The one big mistake that everyone made in the '60s was this idea that everyone could make it. Quite obviously everyone cannot.'

So, there he is, knowingly one of the chosen few, putting his neck where his

Le Mack, le journal et le Man Himself.

mouth is, doing benefit records for the striking miners (The Council Collective's *Soul Deep*), doing surrogate Philly soul 45s like *Shout To The Top* whose video featured him and Mick and DC Lee running through the tune before a mural depicting the courageous heritage of mining communities. He does gigs for CND and walks with the masses on their demos – sure it's good for his image, but nobody says he has to. He does his bit for international youth year. He liaises with Trade Unions against Norman Tebbit's Youth Training Scheme, a sham affair for keeping school leavers out of the unemployment figures. He joins Billy Bragg and Junior Giscombe in the Red Wedge group, entertainers pledged to helping Labour win the next election.

Like it or not Paul is part of the new pop flock; but he's one black sheep who kicks and bleats for all he's worth. As corporations and self-created celebrities work together to capture some magic combination of shock value, playability, credibility, 'personality' and total market crossover, Paul Weller steps outside the territory we're told is entertainment's proper place. He doesn't fit. He's not that *good* at commerce. Maybe part of what's best about Paul is that he sometimes gets it wrong.

For instance, he's not been *too* hot on haircuts. That crypto suedehead (circa '71) effort was acceptable, if quaint, but the floppy fringe job of '84/'85 was just a little hard to take. It coincided with a trough of sartorial caprice involving chequered trousers, a jet black blazer and a matching paisley tie and hankie set with decorative watch chain. It didn't seem like camp, or parody. But if plain eccentric was what it was, what a *wonderful* relief.

'I wouldn't call ours a glossy image,' ponders its creator; 'I suppose it is sophisticated, or at least it tries to be, and that goes along with how I feel about style and clothes and graphics. And I think that's what most working-class kids at least try to aim for. I mean, look at all those soulboys and label boys. Whether you like it or not is irrelevant. That is their attempt at sophistication. It's the same thing as when I was twelve or thirteen and we were all trying to be skinheads or suedeheads. I think the Style Council represent a bit of that as well.'

At one time Paul Weller wanted to bring the Mod dream back, revved up, but completely intact. He's still living half inside that pill-popping 1960s romance, but he's lent its cornered rat fury an articulacy it never had before. His success as a mohair revisionist shows how deeply rooted that culture is in England and how perceptions of it have changed. The Mod boy turned into a Habitat man or a bone head boot boy. In the years that spawned him – a period of Union Jack affluence and Stars and Stripes Cultural imperialism – to be young was to be special in itself. Twenty years later, to be young is to be a discipline problem.

Weller's solution, worked out with painstaking care, and a melting idealism, is to update the Mod myth for the modern world. His own work with Talbot is the logical end product of a Mod manifesto appropriately aged for a man now past 25. His record label, Respond, was an attempt to save the council estate Teen from extinction. Eager youngsters like Tracie Young and the Questions looked like they came straight out of sports outfitters and Chelsea Girl. Their record's bear sleeve notes which are facsimiles of the prose style and street jargon found in Colin MacInnes' London novels, of which the bitter sweet, painfully optimistic *Absolute Beginners* is the most famous and an enduring Weller influence.

Watching Weller wrestle with his present, his inspirations and his past can be a frustrating pastime – I mean, what kind of easy bargain do you *expect* Leon Trotsky to strike with Billy Liar? – but rewarding when it works. *Our Favourite Shop*, the second Council album (summer '85) was the best realisation of their catholic kaleidoscope yet. Their music found a clipped composure that finally transcended pastiche and enabled the 'message' songs to carry the weight of their invective, and slow-burning rage; and the love songs to finally pick the padlock of your heart. It's not without its flaws; but the passions that caused them are, at the same time, the saviour of the best. That, surely is why Weller continues to count. The parameters of pop 'perfection' become more restricting all the time – but Paul's a man with bigger dreams for sale.

I'll buy that capuccino, Kid.

HOWARD JONES
A Mouse With A Grouse

A lot of people really love Howard Jones. He makes their insides go all warm. They feel befriended, encouraged, jollied along. The thing with Howard is that he's so incredibly *elementary*. It's certainly the reason for his success as a personality of pop. Other sensitive (fairly) young men have learned how to make bright tunes with drum machines and synthesisers, but Howard is the special one because he wants to hold your hand. Deep down, people are increasingly frightened and confused by what goes on around them. Howard simplifies the problem. Howard tells them to come out of their shells and make pearls of themselves; if we all look on the bright side and stop being nasty, Howard says, then everything will be all right again.

That's what Howard Jones says, and, of course, he's right. It's the plain fact that Howard stands for such friendly, sensible things that makes him perhaps the best-loved of all the cuddly toy boys of modern pop. This is a relatively new species of Top Forty creature, although, try as we might, we can hardly ignore that fellow Elton John. In recent times, there's been little Nik Kershaw, who is definitely one. So are Curt and Roland of Tears For Fears if we look closely at them. There's no doubt that Phil Collins is another, though his foray into dozey LA machismo with Philip Bailey rather blotted his copybook. Then there's talented Morrissey of the Smiths. Any suggestion that he belongs in this company would upset poor Stephen terribly – so let's say he does, even if it's not true (and, actually, it isn't).

But it's Boy George who is to blame. It was he who introduced furry friend consciousness to beleaguered Britain. A lot of little children and fun-loving grandmas overlooked the sharp side of George's nature which made him so much more than just a lap dog. They saw only the bright clothes and bows and sexlessness, heard and hummed the tunes. Howard embodies precisely that part of George's legacy. He is cuddly, and that is that. It's not a loser quality when placed within the kind of parochial, homespun British cultural oeuvre that nurtures tales of country vets and little hedgerow animals that talk. There's a touch of this in Howard. There are even those who reckon Howard is a field mouse dressed up.

Apart from all this (and lest we forget) Howard also has a winning way with a tune. You've got to admit, those Jonesy jingles really stick. It's a skill which, for years, Howard could be witnessed honing to perfection in little bars and pubs in and around his quiet home counties hometown of High Wycombe most notably in a grubby pub called the Nag's Head.

As time went on, Howard's gigs there had to be stopped for safety reasons – the

Wardrobe by Jeff Banks – but Howard is still the People's Friend.

crowds became so big and boisterous. Howard is proud to be a man of ideals, and when his local fame as a one-man synthesiser band reached so formidable a stage, he could say he had achieved one of them.

Howard had opted out of music college in Manchester at the age of 21. The tutors there were all very classically oriented, it appears, rather narrow-minded when it came to revolutionaries. Howard, more of a free-thinking sort of person, departed disillusioned, and found he had just as many problems meeting the kind of musicians he could create with in a meaningful way. Then someone lent him a clapped-out Bentley drum machine. Suddenly, a little voice spoke to Howard: 'It's better if you do it on your own,' said the little voice. So Howard did.

For Howard, it seems, this decision is integral to his self-definition as a bit of a rebel. 'Pure synth stuff was quite unusual anyway, but I wanted to *do* something, I wanted to make the one-man ideal work,' he later explained; 'you don't *have* to have pre-conceived ideas about how music's going to be presented. You don't *have* to have a funny name. You write the rules, and then you do it.'

This is a cornerstone of Howard's philosophy of life, one he expresses directly through the lyrics of his songs. When Howard signed up to the giant multi-national corporation WEA, pundits took one look at his haircut, listened to his philosophy (outlined in some slightly *obvious* songs) and dismissed him as yet another corporate cock-up – no-one would go for this bit of fluff. *New Song*, the very first Howard Jones single, promptly went to number three in August 1983. Defiantly, Howard sang that he didn't want to be hip or cool. It was the last thing he needed to fret about.

Every tastemaker with pretensions to seriousness thought Howard Jones is a twit. It's not hard to see why. If there were two things which had gone out of style, they were overt protest songs and sheer open-heartedness. Howard guilelessly, shamelessly, piled on both at once. As a social commentator, Howard's analysis was perhaps the shallowest in the history of . . . well, anything. At 28 (so he said, though some maintain he fibbed – unthinkable of course), he sounded as if he'd just read a kind of Penguin Guide to Non-Conformity ('Bourgeois Hegemony: Why It's Simply Horrid') and set it to music. The melody to *New Song* was impossibly cheery, vaguely derivative, and diabolically infectious. Howard cropped up in the teeny press, looking like a cartoon example of the impact of Punk on street theatre types, what with his rhubarb coif, baggy pants and bright red bumper boots. His message was to free your mind! Just like that! People seemed to like it. They liked his second single as well. *What Is Love?*, a cascading piece of Peaudouce existentialism, made number two in November. The video, filmed in moody blue Paris, featured Howard yearning moderately in a cute hat, black and white checked shirt and a long dark coat. He was more of a sweetie than ever. The Christmas issue of *Smash Hits*, Britain's biggest selling pop magazine, had Howard's picture on the front. 'Why Is This Man Smiling?' it demanded. Because readers had voted Howard '83's Most Promising Newcomer, that's why. A twinkling little star was born.

Now thrust into the limelight, a fuller picture of the Jones boy began to emerge. He was similar to the other pin-ups in one way, in that he had very strong opinions about himself. But what made Howard different was what these opinions were. The smirking beauties of the 'new pop' were uniformly clever dicks, crafting double-edged confections with an intellectual touch. Howard, on the other hand, was just plain wide-eyed: 'I wanted to do something that was difficult,' he explained; 'something that would take every ounce of ingenuity I've got, and would really push me forward as a person, because that's what's important.'

Yes, Howard understood the limitations of the material life. He knew about intolerance too – it made him jolly cross: 'looking like I do is a bit of a statement really, because when you walk down the street, and people give you funny looks, you're constantly reminded of what a bigoted world we live in.' And that's another thing: 'the only way people know how to behave is by trying to conform to something, so they're safe; so they don't have to go out and *risk* anything.'

Howard Jones considers his career to be all about taking risks. In Howard's opinion, having a haircut like a West Highland terrier was taking a risk, even though such things had been commonplace on British high streets for years. Howard felt the same about that military green and vermilion boiler suit affair he occasionally wore, also those great lurid oversize fluffy jumpers that became one of his first stylistic trademarks. The clothes were just another part of Howard's statement. He had 'something to say'.

It was intriguing that Howard chose to present himself as a renegade spirit, especially as someone who'd got himself a deal with one of the most conservative of the major companies (WEA missed out badly with Punk). This was a strange kind of rebel whose protestations seemed so untouched by cynicism or rage, so downright . . . *accommodating*. The politeness of Howard's urgings on his first album, *Human's Lib*, rendered hard bitten types working on music magazines speechless. The public, though, put it into the album chart at number one.

Jones' receipt of glory was a tribute to his sheer, unforced consumer appeal. It was a very *pure* kind of success. He had a manifesto for personal growth enshrined in his material, but he didn't turn up trumpeted as the figurehead for some new movement or tendency. The tabloid newspapers, who'd been salivating after Boy George, Steve Strange and the gang even before they went fully public, could find no titillating splash-scandal angle on the Wycombe wonderman, and to this day they have managed to make only the tiniest smear on his perfectly uncorruptible character. It happened in January 1984 when a man called Bill Bryant, who'd written some of the words on *Human's Lib*, claimed he had been 'tossed aside' by Howard once the Jones had tasted fame. The *Sun* reported that Howard had told Bill to 'get knotted'. Two weeks later, the *Sunday People* described how Howard, Bill, Howard's wife Jan and Bill's wife Mandy had been part of an 'Inner Peace sect', which 'made them specially close.' Nudge! Nudge! Mandy had left Bill the day after Howard said 'get knotted' to him, according to the *Sun*, as if that was somehow Howard's fault. Both papers claimed an 'exclusive'. No-one believed them anyway. Howard wasn't that sort of person.

You see, ordinary folk liked the look of Mr Jones, and they enjoyed his chirpy tunes. Howard had plenty of those. He'd spent six years accumulating equipment, refining his stage act, building his local following, and writing his songs. During this time he'd worked in a cellophane factory, given piano lessons, and even done a fruit and veg round with Jan. Then, one day, he was talent spotted by Mike Hawkes, a Radio One producer who lived nearby. It was Hawkes who got Howard his very first session on David 'Kid' Jensen's mid-evening weekday show, which, before Jensen left the BBC for Capital, was probably the most influential programme when it came to breaking new names. The session proved to be a turning point in Howard's long, tiring, unfashionable career.

Once Howard started to become a celebrity, the way he was so *everyday*, so totally unsensational, meant he stuck out like a sore thumb. Even his very significant grass roots following set him apart. His was very much the old-fashioned way. 'I thought if I couldn't get people interested in me in my home town without any records or promotion, then I wouldn't be able to do it on a large scale,' he said, sensibly. And, like it or not, Howard has always been the People's Choice. His weekly gigs at the Nag's Head became almost riotous affairs. As he began getting dates at old-school rock venues like Wardour Street's Marquee, coachloads of supporters followed him down from Buckinghamshire. All this simply contributed to his image as the synthesiser star next door. Howard was unflinchingly amiable: 'I believe the way to change people's attitudes is to be non-pushy,' he said to the pop papers, seemingly sensing no tangiential contradiction between this and his record company's loud declarations that *it* was going to be very pushy indeed. It was going to be putting 'all its marketing muscle' (*Music Week* 3/3/84) behind his Rupert Hine-produced debut LP. Jones' capacity for remaining blithely oblivious to a million inconsistencies seemed total. For sure, he has been blessed.

When you meet Howard Jones, he isn't quite what you expect. Perhaps he anticipates hostility from people with creases in their trousers, but the impression is of a rather bitter, angry individual who's more than a little on the defensive. It is clear – and perfectly reasonable – that he wants to be loved.

Howard Jones' quest is the creation of concord. In his work he tries to show people that this isn't so difficult as it seems. He sends us little revelations: we are *conditioned*; we are all *equal*; we could be free if we only stopped enslaving one another. Howard says it's all a question of attitude. He is unimpressed by notions of irreconcilable vested interests or any of that stuff. To involve yourself in such things is to be part of the herd, and that's definitely bad. Howard asks us all to rally round and *not* be part of the herd together. He wants to engender harmony among his fellows, based on intimacy with himself.

What's so startling is the extent to which he manages it. Jones' concerts are like community gatherings. He's Cliff's closest rival yet in this respect. People of all ages turn up and seem to think of Howard as their friend. On his first big tour he left forms on all the seats, so that people could write their own reviews and send them to him. That's Howard's attitude to a 'T'.

There are no other chart types with whom Howard can be convincingly compared. The other cuddly toy stars are too solidly professional and cool. Howard doesn't wave his crotch at teenage girls like Spandau Ballet do, he doesn't try to dazzle us with techno-chic like Duran Duran, or wink and nudge like George O'Dowd. Instead, he gets all worked up and actually *hops about*. (Oh yes he does!) This is no condescending power posture. Howard is not worshipped, nor does he require it. He wants to say 'thank you' to the people who've made him matter, and you *know* he really means it.

Just before Christmas, 1983, Howard told *Look-In*, the magazine for young pubescent girls, that his ambition was 'to write music and lyrics that are of use to people in some way.' He appears to have managed it. In February 1985, just before his second album (his third if you count the 12-inch re-mix LP) *Dream Into Action* came out, he did an interview for *Just Seventeen*. Question: 'What sort of fan letters do you get?' Answer: 'I don't get anyone saying "I love you, I love you," but that's wonderful. I get incredible letters saying "your song made me feel encouraged when I was feeling down". After I've just read an interview, slagging me off, I'll go through the letters,' continued Howard; 'at the end of the day, it's what the fans think that really matters.'

And at the end of the day, he's right. You can't argue with it, any more than you can argue with the fact that every Howard Jones single has reached the top ten except *Hide And Seek*, which stopped at number twelve. There are around 12,000 people enrolled in the Howard Jones fan club. They are communicated with on a chummily irregular basis via the famous *Risk* fan magazine. This has itself grown from a slightly shabby A5 offset litho effort into an attractive A4 affair of twenty pages with spot colour and lovingly-detailed accounts of what's happened to

Howard and his friends since the last edition.

Inside *Risk*'s pages, and in Howard's down-market magazine interviews, we can familiarise ourselves with the people closest to him, those who've helped him in his career. There's Jed Hoile the mime artist, who adds an extra visual dimension to the live shows. We meet also Mike Roarty, Howard's sound engineer. Always ready with a few helpful tips is Mike. Then there's Mike's wife Jill who helps look after the fan club, and cooks vegetarian meals for everyone when they're off on tour. Most of all, we meet Jan, Howard's wife. She looks after clothes and make-up and is in charge of the fan club.

One of the things Howard likes about Jan is that she doesn't smother him. 'She isn't too clinging,' as he puts it. Howard revealed to *Look-In* that he used to have lots of erotic dreams, but now they're all about Jan (a remark which Jan might take in more ways than one). Most of these people started out as Howard's fans. Now they are parts of the family Jones. Howard's personal philosophies pervade all these personalities of his now mythic private life. *Risk 6* has a recipe for vegetable curry (jokes about vegetarians are one of the few things Howard says he will not stand for – he's made this perfectly clear), and you can get a collection of 'Veggy Recipes' through the fan club for 50p. And those famous Howard Jones jumpers? Why, they're knitted by his sister-in-law, of course.

Success has not desecrated the bounteous optimism of Howard Jones, at least, not so you'd notice much. His single *Like To Get To Know You* was written with the 1984 Olympic Games in mind. The message was that if they just tried a little bit harder, people of all countries and races could really get along. It went to number four, and the Los Angeles Olympiad has gone down in history as the most jingoistic since Hitler hosted the event in 1936.

Lesser men would have been destroyed. But not Howard. His next single (number six, February '85) had another message for us: *Things Can Only Get Better*. Howard was encouraging us again, and, well, you had to admit, there was a core of truth in the sentiment. Just a little *understated* maybe.

Can this man Jones really be the first utterly uncynical pop star? With the album *Dream Into Action* we found Howard encouraging us some more. It was 'about putting your ideals into action and not being an armchair philosopher'. It entered the UK album chart at number one, as if we'd expected anything different. Certainly, though, its contents marked a progression from *Human's Lib*. The 'one man band ideal' was now a thing of the past. The sound was altogether fatter, with backing singers, a horn section, a drummer and a bass guitarist called Martin Jones – yes, he's one of Howard's brothers.

There had been a change too in Howard's haircut, a slight progression from 'cockatoo pop star' (the *Sun*), to a kind of Mohican grow-out. The general tone was of mild progression, an album which still liked to ask the listener nicely ('I don't like the idea of being pushy and offending people,' Howard had once said), but with moments which almost approached unfriendliness. The track *Assault And Battery* was a genuinely pointed attack on the slaughter of animals for food. The Smiths had just released their *Meat Is Murder* album, proving that vegetarianism is indeed one of those subjects around which all shades of pop liberals and radicals could unite. Live and let live. It might sound mealy, but it really matters to Howard Jones. For the first time he came up with a track that *hurt*.

It was the very fact that *Assault And Battery* stands out which proves Howard to be the crown prince of non-controversy. Even his admirers in the pop papers have to admit that he can be a bit of a wet one. Howard has required no taming, has inspired little in the way of moral backlash. But there is something refreshing about a regular chart contender who has received no hysterical hyperbole to help him to the top.

What is Love? Easy! Love is what we feel for Howard.

People just like him. He fulfils a need. Maybe it's something to do with order, simplicity, a primitive dot-to-dot sort of morality. Even the *Guardian* thought he was bland.

Howard went to the Isle of Wight pop festival in 1971, and, if now was then, he'd be a hippy with an acoustic guitar. John Sebastian, maybe. Howard is only a pop star and not a caring flower person because Pop is where today's young perennials have to be. The Dream Academy for example. Today's underground is, after all, a lot more wild. What Howard does instead is present us with a game plan for happiness in which all points of conflict are reconciled. Alternative folk in the old days thought that the innocence of childhood, if cherished and preserved, could be brought to bear on the troubles of the world. Play power was the key.

Howard Jones, in his looks and his songs and his prognostications, has re-assembled this tradition for the shopping precinct age. His solutions grow out of something resembling a ten-year-old's non-comprehension of persistent human failings. Did he really think issuing his song *Equality* in South Africa would encourage wicked white people to change their minds?

Perhaps in the end it's not the messages that Howard sends as the fact that he wants to send them. His compositions are so infectiously enthusiastic, and a lot of people are too scared to be sceptics any more. Maybe there's just something irresistibly attractive about a grown man who can so blithely give Humanity a vote of confidence when so much evidence screams that we deserve no such thing.

In his very first video, the one for *New Song*, we saw Howard followed by gaggles of schoolkids and factory workers through the corridors of Holborn tube station, and out into the sunshine. It remains the perfect metaphor for the man. Howard Jones is a signpost saying, 'this way to a much nicer world.' It's a dead end, of course. But there's plenty who are happy to put that out of their minds. They want to take the joyride just the same.

9

MICHAEL JACKSON
Somewhere Over The Rainbow

Popular wisdom has it that Michael Jackson is halfway round the twist. But if it's true, he seems to be handling it all right. Maybe it's the rest of us who need help.

It clearly is not healthy that someone – anyone – should be as famous as Michael Jackson is. But isn't it even less healthy that many millions of western consumers should have put him where he is? Is it not a terrifying thought that Michael's rise to near omnipotence has progressively become less and less to do with his music, or the image he presents, and more and more to do with the craziness around him?

And what craziness it is. While the frail young man himself pursues his mythical off-duty Lifestyle-In-Wonderland, the world's media projects to us a phenomenon comprised almost entirely of chit chat and sales figures – low speculation and envy, by any other names. The rock biz went bonkers when it learned that over 40 million copies of his 1983 album *Thriller* had been bought, making it easily the biggest selling record of any kind, ever. All over the trade papers full page ads appeared. In them other stars and giant corporations thanked Michael for what he'd done – putting fire into the industry's belly once again. The March 19th 1984 issue of *Time* magazine carried Michael on its cover, and devoted nine whole pages to a feature on him. They didn't even have an interview. When Jackson and five of his brothers went on their 'Victory' tour of America in the summer of '84, two million people paid ten million dollars to see them. An Italian TV company put together a documentary on Quincy Jones a couple of years ago. Jones, a colossal figure in American music himself, produced the *Thriller* album; so more than half the programme's time was devoted to Michael instead. When Michael's eldest brother Jermaine (who stayed on with mighty Tamla Motown to go solo when the rest of the family moved to Epic) visited Britain in 1984, every leisure magazine and newspaper showbiz column was filled with what Jermaine had to say . . . about Michael. A few reporters, including yours truly, were genuinely interested in Jermaine's own work. Jermaine got us off the subject as quickly as he could. 'I have dreamed of being back on stage with my brothers,' he breathed in a kind of devotional daze; 'Michael is the lucky one at the moment. He has been blessed.' Jermaine knew what was best for his career.

Everyone has a Michael Jackson story. The one about Pepsico is a personal favourite. The manufacturers of Pepsi Cola invested more than $5.5 million sponsoring the Jacksons' tour. Michael appeared in two TV commercials for the product. As we know, it was during the making of these that he had the accident

Michael Jackson – model American statesman.

with his hair. When the two massively-publicised ads finally appeared, they were so successful that Pepsico dipped into their pockets again. Not to make more Jackson ads, but to book magazine space telling people what time to tune in and see the original two. All this when to every fan's common knowledge, Michael Jackson doesn't even drink the stuff! But so what? In the July '84 edition of *Advertising Age*, the chairman of Pepsi's ad agency, BBDO, was quoted thus in relation to product endorsement by pop acts: 'This is lifestyle advertising, not a testimonial. What's relevant is what these groups stand for and what their sponsors hope to stand for by tying in with them.'

What Michael stands for is everything that's proud to be American . . . again. He is the first American icon of sheer leisure consumerism. Michael is not about breaking the rules, he is about making them work for you. As *the* figurehead of '80s popular culture, he is completely different to predecessors of comparable impact. Elvis Presley turned poverty music – country and rhythm and blues – into the territory of serious commerce. His was the sound of a new kind of cash flow and a new kind of thrill. Eight years later, the Beatles made the brand new beat into the pulse of Britain's promised wave of affluence. Northern urchins with an upstart charm, they took life in their easy stride, they became a focus for the idealism of the young western world.

Presley and the Beatles were irreverent, optimistic figureheads in an era of discovery and change. Michael is not the same. In his art there is no outwardly-directed rebellion, or even particular innovation. Though Jackson's background was humble, it was also steeped in showbusiness values. The Jackson Five were not a gang of rough-cut delinquents who Tamla Motown gathered up and 'civilised' in entertainment's name. Berry Gordy's empire simply finished off the job. The boys' dad, Joe, had already devoted himself to building their lives in the spotlight, the brightest he could find. His hard work was a homage to an American Way of salvation; an old-fashioned, pre-rock'n'roll, traditional Hollywood American way.

At seven years old (and sometimes at 3am) Michael and his elder siblings were wowing crowds in night-clubs all over Indiana, paying their way, taking the rough with the smooth. By the time they made their first 45 for Motown in 1971 any stray guttersnipe edges had been polished clean away. *I Want You Back* – a teen fizz refinement of Sly Stone's freaky Frisco frenzy – went to number one in the States, number two in the UK, and remains one of the greatest pop records ever made. Two more firecracker singles ensued – the precocious *ABC*, the preposterous *The Love You Save* – and Michael was a heartthrob at eleven. By the time he'd turned 14 he was a millionaire – a total product of the dream machine from the second he entered the world.

Unlike those earlier Godheads of speeding, spendthrift youth, Michael didn't kick against his background or upturn old-hat conventions about what entertainment was supposed to be. He was weaned on those conventions and observed the way they mingled with the new, exultant beat. While still a pre-teen unknown, Michael, with his brothers, was singing support to the mightiest names in black music at the Apollo Theater in Harlem, the culture's holiest shrine. They opened for Jackie Wilson who combined a swooping R&B vocal style with a gleaming supperclub presentation. From the wings they watched with awe the fulminating, pulverising James Brown, the man with the entourage and regular MC, the flashest and the funkiest showman on Earth.

Those were incendiary times, but the boys were very young, and by the time they were ready to seize a piece of history for themselves, the coarse, tough strut of rhythm and blues had long transformed completely into the velvety textures of Soul. Kicked, battered, and finally gunned down, black power eased off into the less combative postures of black pride. There was gold in them there ghettos, and a growing black bourgeoisie as well. So, as the curtain rose on the '70s, the music went through a period of pessimism, then levelled off into the whipped cream finish of Gamble and Huff, the progressive Right On epics of Norman Whitfield, shedding en route the quiet paranoia of the Undisputed Truth's 'Smiling Faces Sometimes' – sometimes don't tell the truth. Meanwhile, in the white world, alternative culture turned into cocaine culture, and that was the end of that.

For magnificent Motown, always at the clean, hit-machine end of the spectrum, the Jackson Five provided the last exuberant shout of their golden age. But as the '70s rolled on the family found themselves looking for a new role to replace the transient teenybop one. It was a struggle. The Jackson clan had always made their ultra white rivals the Osmonds look like the plain, pasty bores they were; the reason was *talent*. But it was a talent that only really worked well when the climate was *frisky*. The '70s didn't suit them. Disco was too camp and frigid for them, and they seemed incapable of making the kinds of records which the white intelligentsia's approval could push into a wealthier market space, as had happened with Marvin Gaye and Stevie Wonder.

Then, in a grand cultural retreat into self-love, America revived Hollywood rules on the right, and built the Body Boom on the left. This was the Jacksons' moment once again. They re-discovered flash and heat and razzle-dazzle sex appeal. Pow! *Shake Your Body* and *Blame It On The Boogie* put the group back in the charts. Suddenly they belonged once again in the modern world. With their album *Triumph* (1980) they stormed into their third decade as fit and lean as they'd ever been. *Triumph* was smooth, it was hypnotic, it was total '80s dance music – textured, layered, precision-built. Much of it was played by co-producer Greg Phillinganes on machines. If it is possible to draw such a line (and some draw it far too easily – ask George Clinton) this wasn't soul music. It was almost pure body music, in that all its passion was funnelled through a scintillating sense of *absolute motion*.

Lyrically, there wasn't much except strings of dance exhortations and facile platitudes to Universal Love. But none of that mattered very much. This was music about two things: groove power, and Michael's squealing, squalling breathless delivery. Here was a man in a hurry. But what was he hurrying from?

From here on, the Michael mythology really begins. The best track on *Triumph* was *Heartbreak Hotel*, a hit as a single, and the only one attributed solely to him. It was a song about being haunted by memories; about fear, paranoia, running away. In March 1980, Michael appeared on the cover of *Melody Maker*, announced by the cover line 'Michael In Wonderland'. Inside we learned, among other things, that Michael considered a highlight of his life to have been singing *When You Wish Upon A Star* on TV, surrounded by cartoon characters from 25 years of Walt Disney. 'In Disneyland you forget about the outside world,' he explained; 'escapism and wonder. . .makes you feel good, it allows you to do things. You just keep moving ahead.'

The rest is history, but it's a different history to those that have gone before. Whether or not Michael has really cracked, we just don't know. But what *is* clear is that the glaze of stardom has remained intact. Most astronomical pop celebrities have either fallen to pieces in private or given in compliantly to the currents which seek to carry them. Presley, the prototype, died a mess, a helpless figure at the mercy of his own reputation. Jagger and McCartney have simply turned into complacent parodies of themselves. John Lennon kicked, screamed, and died a very literal victim of his own fame.

Jackson, on the other hand, has simply carried on. His retreat from the world has not been an escape, just a move deeper into the territory that has always been his home. What for others came as culture shock, for Jackson has been merely culture concentration. He went public before he knew what the word meant. What else is there for him to do but stay there?

In this, Michael is the perfect symbol for Born Again America. He believes totally in what those saccharine tour guides at University City call 'the sheer *magic* of entertainment'. He is a study of a man sticking close by his faith, through all the ups and all the downs as well. The suffering is not a cause for disillusion; it is just the natural flipside of success. You put up with it. It doesn't undermine your *raison d'être*.

This is the crunch point with Michael. We like to hear stories about how, by most people's standards, he has lost his marbles, but his funny little ways are not seen as part of some desperate secret, they are accepted as an aspect of his winner's appeal. The weird stuff is now the norm. It doesn't spoil the picture any more. In the counter-culture years people spied a beast at the heart of the Hollywood dream and tried to hunt it down, but now they want Hollywood back and they want it *warts and all*. They want kick ass and razzamataz, and they voted for an old screen cowboy who forgets half his lines, but whose timeless West Coast poolside machismo matters more. No-one thought much of his policies, they just kinda liked his style. To hell with everything else. He may be a fool but he's *our* fool, as Randy Newman sang of Lester Maddox. Bring back the big screen; it's sure beats no screen at all.

Enter Michael in star-spangled glory. He had something for everyone. Affluent America wanted to look good and stay young, and not too much more. Young America wanted non-stop Disneyworld. Middle-aged America wanted a return to the values of yore. Michael gave them all what they wanted. He gave them *Off the Wall*. With this tingling, sizzling, half-possessed, half-frivolous LP, Michael re-introduced himself as the embodiment of all the *right* things to be. He was hot, fit and funky. He was innocent, unspoiled. He was religious – a devout Jehovah's Witness. He was familial – one of those nice Jackson boys. He wasn't about to feed off or provoke any difficult stuff like social unrest. And boy, could he take care of business. Seven million albums worldwide. Hey!

So what if the kid was nuts? The America that made Richard Nixon a chat show star reaches out for Michael Jackson because it's just like touching base, a base that's all the more solid because the cuckoo land that lies behind the professional poise is so clearly perceived. It is now expected that political leaders are crooks, and it is expected that entertainers are either megalomaniacs or half mad. Now America has got over the shock, it just makes its icons more real, more reliable, and this adds credence to the most important thing of all – that Michael is the biggest and the best.

With *Thriller*, Michael just sealed the last part right up. The album is a jigsaw puzzle. Each piece is a separate, but crucial, part in the epic phenomenon, but what's most symbolic of all is that *Thriller* is secretly a bitter pill coated in sugar.

On the title track, Jackson again acts out his terror, but his point of reference is an adolescent horror movie, complete with Vincent Price. Rod Temperton wrote the track, but Michael picked it for inclusion out of hundreds of submitted candidates. The album's opener, *You Wanna Be Startin' Something*, and the pent-up, punchy *Beat It* with its street fighter metaphor are both Jackson compositions, and the distinguished soul writer Gerri Hirshey was swift to spot their cornered, defensive essence in the course of a piece for *Rolling Stone* published just after the album's release. 'They demand that, and they want this,' Jackson told her; 'they think that they own you, they *made* you. If you don't have faith, you go crazy.'

Jackson's faith is in the power of music as a means of escape, a way to 'get out of yourself', as Ms Hirshey has noted; a way to make the whole world smile. *Thriller*,

Michael and nervous interested parties captured at Madame Tussauds by David Corio.

emotionally and musically eclectic, is the ultimate crossover item. The nine tracks glide through romance, anger, vengeance, pain and pleasure; through schmaltz, hard rock, Afro-funk, mainstream modern dancefloor soul and pop. There's material for working out and some for cooling off. *The Girl Is Mine*, a gushing duet with Paul McCartney, is a joint celebration of the dream of innocence and the community of showbiz, the only one where Jackson can function as a social animal; megastars are his only friends. Quincy Jones and James Ingram's *PYT (Pretty Young Thing)* is a burst of romantic optimism. *Billie Jean* is Jackson's own, another hunted tale of accusation and denial. Its creeping, predatory backbeat is one of the best and most pervasive grooves of modern times, while the track's underlying theme – a fear of female demands – has given Freudian analysts of Michael Madness a field day.

As a sharp piece of commercial contemporary soul, *Thriller* has, as Quincy Jones said, put black American music back in the pop charts where it belongs, and where it has enjoyed only a tenuous residence since the first Jackson invasion. But, in the end, the ecstatic interest surrounding it was very little to do with music, and everything to do with Michael.

A deeply conservative record – sentimental, moralistic, and running scared – *Thriller* took off like a rocket. In 1983, the entire capitalist world moved to the rock flash and lean groove of *Beat It* and *Billie Jean*. (I checked in to a cheap hotel in Mexico City during November of that year. I switched on a tiny pocket radio. Guess what I heard played back to back?) Everyone seemed to unite around this painfully shy forced recluse from Gary, Indiana, who now lived with his mum, dad and sisters in the San Fernando valley. Michael posed on the cover with his brand new aquiline nose job, an unexpectedly slender mouth, cheekbones prominent, and with the Afro coiffure of yesteryear glossed and tweaked and teased back behind his ears. A tiger cub plays on his knees. Introducing Mr Young and Universal, a Michael out of Michelangelo's dreams.

From now on, celebrity seized the reins and galloped into immortality. Michael's unprecedented surge to absolute stardom saw him utterly outstrip his brothers, isolating him in the public eye, and so lending the doings of the Jackson dynasty still more of the sickly smell of soap. Mass approval of Michael's moral standards was cosseted still further by the common public knowledge that he only agreed to do the Victory tour for the sake of his sibling former partners' somewhat insignificant careers. Even Jermaine, newly signed to Arista, was let back into the fold for the extraordinary cross-country itinerary and the record which preceded it.

The *Victory* album turned out to be a painstaking exercise in democracy (or should that be positive discrimination?). Songwriting credits and lead vocals were religiously shared out among the six of them, except that it's Michael who opens and closes the show. Everything in between veers between the unremarkable and the awful. The cover art, an illustration by Michael Whelan, was commissioned by Michael because he liked the book jacket Whelan had done for sci-fi author Isaac Asimov's *Foundation's Edge*. He identified with the sense of alienation, Whelan said. Everyone posed for the drawing except Michael. He sent a photograph instead.

The entire Victory circus kept the world's media happy for weeks on end. Rabidly, they tore into rumours of inter-family scraps about promoters and percentages and *dis*organisation. *Newsweek* covered the tour's opening from their front page. *People Weekly* devoted a cover to the 'Behind The Scenes Frenzy' which preceded the event. Every British national newspaper sent someone along to the opening night at the Arrowhead Stadium in Kansas City, to get some determinedly sceptical angle on the biggest rock phenomenon in twenty years.

Yes, that's *rock* phenomenon. Victory was about cash, cash, personality clashes and cash. Jackson was an emphatically mainstream figure, far too household a name to bear the epithet 'soul'. It was decided that there was nothing 'ethnic' about this boy any more. Anyone who'd made that much money and kept his mouth shut just *had* to be, save in the most literal sense, 'white'. Michael had crossed over musically all right, but more than that he crossed over *financially*.

That was the marvellous thing about Michael. He papered over the cracks. The extent of his success in this can be gauged by the blunders of those who were slowest off the mark. Everyone continues to deny it like mad, but the story of how MTV only played the *Billie Jean* video after CBS (Epic's parent company) threatened to withdraw all promos by all their other artists, persists. *Billie Jean* is one of *Thriller*'s 'blacker' tracks. Now, of course, anything by Michael is a very big deal, and clips by rock-oriented or more 'theatrical' black artists – Eddy Grant or Grace Jones – are readily shown, squeezed into the 'New Music' mould. But when in early '84 a story surfaced that a second McCartney/Jackson duet had been shelved because some of the ex-Beatle's middle-class caucasian audience weren't too happy with this, er, 'ethnic' association, it gave the game away again. *The Girl Is Mine* had been a hit, and Paul and Stevie Wonder had made number one with *Ebony and Ivory*. You couldn't mistake the sentiment (being the operative word) of *that*. But, though the gesture had been made, a gesture it seemed, was enough, because gestures are what it's all about.

Michael's career since *Thriller* has comprised entirely of making gestures. According to a survey in *People* (which exists for this kind of thing) he earned seventy million dollars during 1984, without even making a record. He didn't make one in 1985 either. So what *has* he been up to? There was the Victory tour, but he gave his share of the profits to charity. In fact, all Michael has really done since *Thriller* is promotion. The tour was promotion-as-entertainment. The singing he did on Rockwell's *Somebody's Watching Me* single (more paranoia – and from Berry

Gordy's son!) and on Jermaine's solo album were just bits of promotion for them, and also telling indications of how Michael is so big, and so invaluable to CBS, that he can do whatever he likes. He promoted himself through Pepsi Cola. He went to the White House to help promote the President's anti-drunk driving campaign, although everyone knew it was really just the start of Ron's ultimately triumphant drive for re-election. He promoted himself and his Disney connection by appearing in the company's limited 3-D production *Captain Eo*, and his Family Of Stars aroma was promoted when Jackie Onassis took control of a planned new Michael biography. This is the kind of thing Michael did. He went around in that surrogate *Sergeant Pepper's* bandsman's outfit, just *being Michael*, just being a symbol of everything everyone *agreed* about. From *Billie Jean* to Band Aid, '80s pop is a healer to compete with Jesus of Nazareth.

Michael is the embodiment of agreement. They say he works so hard at taking the bad news out of his life that he never, ever looks at the front pages of newspapers. Well, who can't relate to that? Everyone agrees to agree about Michael so much that they even agree to accept all the horrors that seem to haunt each second of his totally unreal life – in fact, by accepting them, they find they agree even more. All these stories about how Michael had rowed with his Dad, went out with boys, was Diana Ross's son, wouldn't talk to his brothers without a lawyer, locked himself in the White House toilet for fifteen minutes when mobbed by domestic staff, took female hormones, talked to dummies, played with robots, and hated *Victory* tour promoter Don King – they were all just part of the way Michael confirmed the positive new outlook. Michael's mystique blends new American fashions with the old American Way, and clinches triumph after triumph from the shadows of what had become the great American Nightmare.

Micheal is not a fantasy in a vacuum like the old stars from before the teenage revolution. He is the manifestation of a fantasy surviving a lunatic reality. Where Bruce Springsteen silhouettes the troubles of today against the romance of yesterday, and Sylvester Stallone kids us that the troubles were never there at all, Michael refutes the heresies of the last thirty years by *handling* them – Michael says the dream took a pounding, but it still gets up and walks. An enduring paradox of his mammoth myth is that he's half the child innocent and half a business perfectionist with a killer streak. The fact that *no-one* is ripping *him* off is widely reported and loudly acclaimed. Michael doesn't want to break the rules or pretend that they're not there. He wants to make believe *and* he wants a nice clean win. From Walt to Rockefeller, Michael puts America back together again.

Meanwhile, back in the fringes of Hollywood, a young black singer watches cartoons, plays with his snake and takes his llama for walks. He looks after himself. Michael knows all about the sharks. They've been there in the bathtub since he left his mother's womb. Corraled by the menacing forces of mass adoration, Michael has done what for him is the natural thing – he's just given in. Michael, the eternal child of showbiz, has turned the price of fame into a multi-media parable of appreciation . . . and he's surviving. In April '85, he came to London to see a brand new waxwork of himself at Madame Tussauds, 'Which one's the dummy?!' smirked the upmarket newsrags, forced to dirty their hands. The answer is us for wanting to ask.

10

::

PRINCE
Of Mushroom Clouds, Myth and Dirty Minds

When it comes to the man who Madonna Ciccone calls 'The Midget', speculation is the thing. It's been like that right from the start in 1978 when a very young man from Minneapolis signed an unprecedented contract with mighty Warner Brothers. He meant nothing outside his hometown. Yet he now had guaranteed backing for three LPs, and, incredibly, complete artistic control. Already he was the object of envy, a pocket-size legend. And by the time the terms of his contract had been honoured, his state of independence would be more than contractual fact – it would be the basis of his giant-sized fiction too.

By 1984 when the former Prince Nelson Rogers finally made the whole world sit up and beg with an album and a feature film, both called *Purple Rain*, fiction and fact would be so tightly tangled in both press and public minds that the difference between them would be virtually irrelevant. And as for enlightenment . . . well, the last place this was likely to come from was the mouth of the *artiste* himself. The tale of Prince's ascent is a classic contemporary showbiz fable – a conspiracy of silence, the central driving force in an absolute escalation of myth.

Once upon a time, enigma was the by-product of popular acceptance, a tangible kind of success. Prince, though, has tied effect so tightly to cause that it is difficult to tell which one is which. He didn't start to make the big time until his mythical substance as a tissue of rumour and outrage had been fixed. For two years he was a strictly marginal interest, a freaky sideshow for teenage blacks who was talented, original even, but basically a gimmick. How else could the kid be explained after a horny adolescent mini-hit called *Soft And Wet*? His debut album *For You* was released to mass commercial disinterest, but never mind. His second, *Prince* spawned a single, *I Wanna Be Your Lover* which mined an established, but neatly executed, electric pop-funk vein, and became a huge soul hit. In a pained falsetto squeak the singer declared that he couldn't bear the subject of his song to pop her cork for anybody else – a demand which lent the tune an air of petulance as much as passion. The LP sold a useful half-million copies in the States and earned a British release. Manchild sexpot was born. With media attention comes media intrusion. This Prince guy was a weird one. Did he *really* play every instrument and write every song? What made him think a cover shot of himself sitting stark naked astride a white horse with wings was a smart way to help shift his LP? Was he sensual and attractive, or slimy and repulsive? What were the facts? What was the truth?

From here on in, every possible resource has been mobilised to prevent us finding

Carnally crazed and depraved perhaps, but God still gets a look in.

out. It is a risky Hollywood staple, but our hero hurled himself gladly onto the casting couch and has been making one huge great movie of himself ever since.

Whether by accident or by design (and who's to know which!) Prince understood what makes a box office hit. His production combined two of the surest money-spinning components: disaster and sex. Dispensing with the management of Owen Husney – the Minneapolis businessman who'd got him his famous deal – he hired instead the hot shot Californian company Cavallo, Ruffalo and Fargnoli, then went off to record a wildly salacious disc called *Dirty Mind*.

Released in 1980, there was nothing remotely coy about its maker's quest. The cover shot captures him with his overcoat undone to reveal nothing but the most truncated item of underwear yet witnessed publically on a male pop artist's person. Five rows of studs decorated the overcoat's right shoulder, and on the left lapel a badge (appropriated from the British 2-Tone label) bore the slogan 'rude boy'.

This was no idle promise. It was difficult to believe you were really hearing some of what came out of the grooves. It wasn't the first time Prince had flaunted his libido in public, but so far he'd been discountable as just a juvenile jerk getting himself steamed up. This, though, was heavy-duty stuff. Prince picked up on all the lascivious doings pop had always liked to *imply* and shouted them out loud. What's more, he added a few of his own. Among his repertoire of overheated tunes nestled sundry tawdry tales of masturbation, incest and oral sex.

There were musical surprises too. *Bambi*, a track on the *Prince* LP, had sounded nothing like a *soul* song. Its hard, square riffs were those of heavy rock, and it turned out to be an omen. The latest Prince sound was a mixture of conventional electric guitars and drums, with ingeniously integrated synth, together conspiring in a new combination of funk and rock.

His image, his noise and his postures were a long way from those dominant in the black musical mainstream at the time. But there was something else as well. Though songs like *Head, Sister, Uptown* and *Do It All Night* retained their adolescent edge – the urge to say a dirty word – they came across as more than mere naughtiness: they were virtual declarations of faith. Then there was *Party Up*. Its high-stepping backbeat was blunt and defiant. So was its lyric. It seemed that Prince and his pals did not want to take up arms – they wanted to take off their clothes.

Hell's teeth! A philosophy of life!

America's intellectual rock pundits – basically a bunch of affable East Coast eggheads and ageing Weatherman sympathisers – had been starved of anything with fire in its belly for God knows how long. But they'd been fascinated by the snarling depressionism of British punk rock, and there was a touch of all that about Prince. 1980 was also the year that Ronald Reagan was swept to power on the wings of the so-called Moral Majority, and *Dirty Mind* took on the aspect of a libertarian stand against the conservative tide. The critics went after Prince like piranhas after live, raw meat.

What then was his message, this youthful messiah who told us that fellatio with virgins was great? Had he *really* done it with his sister? Was hedonistic abandon *seriously* the antidote to all that brand new talk about the Draft?

A picture, hazy round the edges but vivid in all the right places, began to emerge. The soft-porn starlet told us he was a poor half-caste from a large muddled family and a broken home. His father was black, his mother a white half-Italian. Dad was a piano player and not very often around. Frequently left to his own devices, or off-loaded onto relatives and friends, the lonely youngster had upped and gone to the nearby home of his friend André when the first pubescent tremors took a hold. André's mum, a less conventional woman than Prince's, had let her son transform their basement into a recreation space all of his own where he and his new friend messed around with guitars and tried to persuade sundry local girls to do unusual things. The friendship lasted, and André – who'd taken the surname Cymone – was now the guitarist in Prince's band.

This was wonderful material. Prince, from being just one of several rising black teen pin-ups in the late 1970s, was suddenly the rock sociologist's dream date, the ultimate mixed-up, messed-up boy on the brink of making good. Then suddenly, the supply of unprocessed data dried right up. Prior to the release of *Controversy*, *Dirty Mind*'s scene stealing follow up, Prince walked out of an interview with *Musician* magazine, and hasn't done another one since.

Crack-up or caprice? No-one can be certain, and no-one is about to upset Himself by trying too hard to find out. But, whatever, it effectively launched the most simple but devastating PR operation of recent hype history.

In the war for acclaim it's the media battleground that counts for most. While the American president is billed 'the great communicator', Prince has adopted the same priorities but turned them inside out. With the walkout, his own battalions were mobilised – that is, they threw down their weapons and hid behind their shields instead. Prince's contention was publicity enough; that God would love America best if everyone sloughed off their responsibilities and hurled themselves actively into non-stop pleasures of the flesh. Having said it, he imposed exile upon himself, and by his isolation became more of a spectacle than ever.

All Prince's career moves from then until *Purple Rain* were perfectly logical extensions of the principle. Musically, he became more and more rock-oriented, and the *Purple Rain* album carries only faint electro-inflected echoes of the funk tradition. The *Purple Rain* movie, meanwhile, is little more than a glamourised, dramatised rehash of those shady childhood tales, tarting up and complicating his myth, fuelling his mystique to ever higher heights. Immune to close inspection, the mystery just perpetuates itself. The entire *Purple Rain* process was simply the total post-rock advertisement – history retouched before our very eyes.

1981's *Controversy* album was Prince's first to be made from a position of bubbling stardom, and it showed. Its self-importance was obvious. Where *Dirty Mind* was an upstart's assertion, *Controversy* was an attempted epic. Prince had Something To Say and there was, at last, an audience ready to hear it.

Self-consciousness in rock manifests itself in lengthy instrumental build-ups. Self-worth in rock manifests itself in self-reference. The album's title track combined both of these in something approaching a funkoid oration, and the trio of songs comprising side one together amount to a regal manifesto. With his very first words, Prince addressed himself complainingly to the speculation he'd attracted. Was he black, or white? Did he fancy boys or girls or both? Bemoaning controversy, in one breath, he whipped up some more with his next: No more rules! No more racial differences! No more underwear!

A work about banner headline frenzy, *Controversy* revelled in it from cover to cover. Prince intoned the Lord's prayer. Prince declared that life was just a game. Prince appointed himself champion of a whole new breed and bade *Ronnie, Talk To Russia*, so regaling the champion of the old. Prince declared that 'sexuality is all we'll ever need'. Prince dissolved the ballad *Do Me Baby* into a string of orgasmic groans. Prince did a song called *Jack U Off*, which the Pope would not have cared for. Prince also mustered nervous rhythms that gave his songs a dangerous punch, but his earnest lyrical indignation lent them too, the comic edge of a thwarted infant's rage. 'Look at me,' it screamed; 'I want to be left alone.'

Controversy remains an impressive album, full of variations, in which 'The Midget' shows off the full range of his undeniable talents. It also reveals the deep conservatism which lies at the core of his world. His vision has been described as that of 'a sexually liberated America', but what Prince has really done is revive the discredited ideas of the so-called 'sexual revolution'.

In practice, this much-trumpeted emergent sexual 'democracy' offered little more than masculine freedom of conquest. No wonder all those hippies turned into cavemen. Nowhere is the proprietorial passion of His Royal Badness more thoroughly pronounced than in his exhortation at the euphoric, er, climax to the sparkling *Private Joy*. This wasn't the hand-job anthem its title suggests. It was about a girl – and make no mistake, she *belonged* to Prince!

The torrent of publicity surrounding Prince's massive success defines him absolutely as a figure of his time. But just as vital to his total conquest of his homeland was the way the pasts and the presents of black *and* white musics were blended into the perfect modern mélange. His strong roots in the 'permissive' age – roots which, typically of today, he is too young to have experienced first hand – lead us to Sly Stone and his Family who burst from the belly of be-laurelled San Francisco to make the theory of racial harmony a fact, if only up on a stage.

But Prince will have been just as aware of the only other 'coloured' face to be accepted by the hippies, that of Jimi Hendrix. Comparisons are obvious and frequently made. The ringlets and ruffles, Edwardian coats and the taste for purple are plainly throwbacks, and the comparisons would soon become musical too, first at the lavish consummation of *Let's Go Crazy* (the opening track on *Purple Rain*) and later with the bizarre and unexpected acid concept of 1985's *Around The World In A Day*.

Rogers Nelson has his ghosts all right. But it's the differences between him and them which really tell the tale. Prince, Stone and Hendrix vaulted consumer racial divides, but only one has profited from enduring racial assumptions. Stone was too shrewdly political; radical, extrovert and tough – and he paid for it. Hendrix was a guitar genius, but had to prostitute his flair to garner the Woodstock people's approval. Forced to pander to their impulse for excess, Hendrix gave the red-eyed white kids what they seemed to want – meandering, endless feedback, and ugly racist legends about big black cocks.

Prince, the product of more jaded and suspicious times, insulates himself from the vacuity of others. He has tucked himself away from drugs and movements. He might be looking for *The Ladder*, but he's first and foremost a career man. He portrays himself as a different, stealthier brand of black exotic, who has tapped the impulse of big-time white pop as well, and sold himself as a cutting combination of both. Prince does not invite nasty suppositions about heroic negro studs. With conventional machismo currency long in fashionable decline, Prince has contrived a kitschy kind of sexuality based on the unresolved, open-ended sensualism of funk. He still threw phallocentric postures when playing live, but he was always much more *delicate* about it. He's the great camp seducer; an eternally elusive dandy without an axe to grind, but with a fairy tale to tell.

With more and more of the monied public in his pocket and a reputation as a brilliant stage performer, Prince proceeded to clinch his ideological coup. In the time-honoured fashion he offered a whiff of forbidden fruit as a kind of escape route into debauchery. Taking the nation's pulse, he made it race by turning the threat of absolute catastrophe into an excuse for total licence, and voicing a lurid certainty; that parties were not meant to last.

Modern America likes to make a melodrama of itself. And with the release of the single *1999* Prince fine-tuned into its mood. *1999* honed the Princely equation, simplifying it into its most potent form yet, re-inventing and feeding off popular clichés of the day: what shall we do between the four-minute warning and the fry-up to end them all? Part hyper-erotic, part frisson of horror and part hopelessly defeatist, *1999* paints a tempting picture of one long, apocalyptic descent into lust. It was funky, it was rocky, it was flash and catchy edgy entertainment. How could it possibly fail?

In the States a double album followed with the huge smash single as its title track. It was the first Prince album not to have its maker's picture on the front, relying instead on the lewd one's patented suggestive lettering. Presumably, the all-important facial profile was established enough.

For Britain the package was trimmed to a single and carried a near full-length shot of the new star looking his most unearthly yet. There were still rude songs, but the 'rude boy' badge was gone. Prince's ambi-sexual image was emphasised with a newly upped Glam factor in keeping with the UK's now established conventions of pop success. The studded purple coat was no longer of a grimy gaberdine. Instead it had a wholly regal lurex finish – Prince broke into Britain as the complete fop monarch from outer space.

In *1999* Prince began to express a kind of fatalist's flipside to his homeland's ongoing political braggadocio. He accepted the Biblical promise of Armageddon at its word rather than wielding it as a threat. Throughout, there ran a sense of deathly resignation to underpin a rabid celebration. Here was a dire, but persuasive, prediction which wholly discounted the possibility of change. *1999* saw a shift in his perspective from crusader to doomed reveller. Join the party now, for tomorrow we shall die.

It's a self-indulgent solution, acted out through the contents of a pretty self-indulgent album. The concept carried a strident contemporary ring, but at its heart lay a convenient defeatism. The title track, with a unique conjunction of funk, rock and synthetics which had evaded even Funkadelic, worked brilliantly. But, elsewhere, Prince walked a fine line between crisp holocaust comedy and low psychosis dignified. Nowhere is this more pronounced than in *1999*'s variations on the old sex-as-saviour theme. *Little Red Corvette* – definitely *not* about a car – was a crotch-clutching parody of substantial charm, but the white-knuckled declarations of *Let's Pretend We're Married* carry an uncomfortable whiff of malice, and *Lady Cab Driver*, an otherwise engrossing minor epic with a clever cosmopolitan jazz-funk groove, turns into a barely subliminal rape scene. This wasn't the only way in which Prince, in attempting to shore up an audience weaned on Van Halen and Kiss, was in danger of capitulating to their own dreary norms. *All The Critics Love U In New York*, smirked the new star on the American set, expressing a perfectly routine star paranoia. Poor little Prince – *Delirious* indeed.

1999 was a giant success in the States and finally broke Prince in the British market as well. From this point on, everything was sacrificed in the name of Fame, as His Royal Badness set his own career story in a solid wall of Soap. The result was that the entire *Purple Rain* saga amounted to little more than one man flaunting the trophies of a game long won. As such, he threatened to render them utterly without worth.

The *Purple Rain* movie, released in the summer of 1984, told us precisely nothing about Prince that we didn't already know – or think we knew. Its purpose seems to have been to preserve its manufacturer in celluloid – a showroom dummy on spools. The film invites us to assume we are watching a dramatised re-run of Prince's True Life Story, although we most certainly are not, if only because two vital figures from his past career are eradicated completely from the script. The primary absentee is André Cymone, who might well be one to scoff at the film's giving-is-receiving moral. He and Prince had fallen out around the time of *Dirty Mind* and his story has been much sought after ever since.

Most of Prince's protégés and entourage play themselves or close approximations, including Morris Day and his then band the Time, all the members of the Revolution (Prince's band) and his personal bodyguard, Charles 'Big Chick' Huntsberry. But Vanity, leader of camisoled camp followers Vanity 6, doesn't show either. She was reported in the US magazine *Rock & Soul* to have walked out on the project before serious filming started after a series of rows. It didn't matter though. The Star had already found a new real-life lover who he wanted to create as his Eve. Patty Kotero, a 24-year old Hispanic former model from Santa Monica, got the job. Prince had her change her name to Apollonia. As such she became the movie's much slapped and manipulated heroine, lead singer of *Apollonia 6*, and no questions asked.

Unsurprisingly, Apollonia has since been comprehensively quizzed about the true nature of the Great Enigma, as are all and any of his associates, present and past. This undignified parade of the spurned, the patronised and the disillusioned did Prince's PR for him in 1984, compounding the Myth still more each time they kissed and told. André Cymone, struggling to launch a solo career with CBS, granted the ill-fated LA-based 'personality' glossy, *Rock Magazine*, an extensive interview, published in two parts in early '84. All the sordid adolescent details were dug out, all the predictable assertions that the young Prince Nelson Rogers had been a nice respectable boy back then, who 'didn't even cuss'. Cymone also claimed joint credit for many of the Purple One's early compositions and for the sales pitch of the *Dirty Mind* phase. Later, Vanity, whose solo album *Wild Animal* made a lot of inquisitive people writhe with embarrassment during the same year, popped up in a Sunday colour supplement, droning on about how she still feels close to her

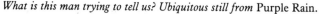

What is this man trying to tell us? Ubiquitous still from Purple Rain.

discoverer, and what a prime performer the five-foot two-inch sleazoid is in the sack. What a way to make a living.

The Purple Rain Process swiftly became a right royal bore. In the film, only the carefully staged live footage contained many thrills, whilst the album was a dull, dense, bombastic affair, littered with brushed-up rock clichés and tired attempts at outrage. The finale of the movie simply confirmed what the entire business conspired to announce – the final arrival of Prince as *the* big name of 1984.

All traces of the former Bomb-consciousness had been purged from both album and film, and right at the beginning Prince is urging us to draw comfort from the prospect of the life beyond. Perhaps this is intentionally the culmination of a career-long allegory for the decline and decimation of Planet Earth. But that's purely academic, since the sole axes of this latest Prince appeal were the libido and the quest for acclaim. On *Let's Go Crazy* he scoffs at Beverly Hills, but his victory chant is a regular showbiz number. *Baby I'm A Star* heralds his entrance into the core of the Hollywood Dream.

Prince's rise to massive popularity has been subjected to a multitude of different analyses. Even Freud has been trotted out, tucked up next to those tales of parental excess, to form the basis of an explanation that it's all a cry for help. But the Purple One's rise has also, irresistibly, been compared and contrasted with that of Michael Jackson, and they are indeed equal and opposite in so many ways. Both are diminutive, private, perfectionist, workaholic, isolated Peter Pan figures. Both made their names as black artists, both now bestride the white market as well. Both imply androgyny and owe much of their status to gender-bent sex appeal.

The differences are just as glaring. Michael is Mickey Mouse risen from the grave, while Prince is disaster movie and skinflick rolled into one. Both have become abstracted, stage-managed figments of human beings. They are distanced obsessions, all the more attractive for their flaws, still more incentive for the diseased desire to pry.

Prince, deliberately or not, has fanned the flames around himself to such an extent that nothing else remains. Movies, gossip, videos, photos, posing, preening, winking – everything is subjugated to the creation of yet more speculation, yet more capitulation to the tinsel allure of the private legend going public without giving anything away. Prince differs from his ancestors mostly in that he didn't first have to lose his grip or die. The myth is all built in. He has constructed an amoral fable of death and damnation and called it a career.

And that's the thing about the Holocaust Threat – it's very good for sales.

Sequel: A Princely Repentance

In the spring of 1985 Prince released his seventh long player and left all and sundry wondering whether the monarch of the purple reign had found *The Ladder* he referred to in one of the album's key songs, or whether he had just gone round the bend. On the other hand maybe he'd just been subjecting himself to too many video re-runs of *Yellow Submarine*.

Around The World In A Day came soused in nothing other than sheer psychedelia. The Hendrix-like axe attacks witnessed on his previous album now blossomed into full-blooded electric hippy jigs and reels. Mutated funk noises mingled with finger cymbals and tambourines. Popping bass lines kept company with elliptical nursery rhyme melodies. The whole lot conspired in what can only be described as the strangest piece of purple philosophising yet, a fantastical display of reaction and repentance, apparently for former sins.

Well, would you believe it? Enclosed within a sleeve recalling the flower child phantasias of a million acid head artefacts, Prince outlined a new innocent's dream of transcending the material world. The route to attaining this superior sense of Being involved enlarging the scope of American 'freedoms' apparently to help keep 'communism' at bay (*America*) and realising that the idyllic home of star-spangled peaceful euphoria, *Paisley Park*, is right there inside us all. It meant doing away with both possessiveness and with drugs. It meant forsaking sinful ways. And right at the end it meant repudiating Lust. On went the epic closing track *Temptation*, the Sleazoid of the Apocalypse rejoices once more in his familiar lasciviousness before finding himself corrected by a deep celestial voice from above: 'Now die!' concludes the voice. The Prince repents and fades away.

On the face of it, here was an astounding reversal from the brash blue arrogance of his initial rise. But in the end where else is there for a megastar recluse to go but inwards? The morality might seem to be entirely reversed, but not really. It's just the same old stuff accommodating the existential ponderings that isolation brings, marked as ever, by the bizarre political equations which seem commonplace among Americans. *Paisley Park* was indeed the logical place for a millionaire misfit to end up. And, for all the slight return to dancefloor R&B with 1986's *Parade*, his spiritual pre-occupations still dominate. It was a psychedelic destination entirely fitting in view of what had gone before. As a parting communication to those who'd been following the plot since he first slithered into the big time, Prince squealed that he didn't know when he'd be back. Many, he had rightly assumed, would await his return – such is the total confidence of knowing people care.

11

::

THE THOMPSON TWINS
Wholemeal Hits The High Street

Everything is pop in the 1980s. I am pop, therefore I am. I am not pop, therefore my hearse awaits. And if you don't think that's true, then what about the Thompson Twins? Ten years ago they wouldn't have been seen *dead* in a book like this.

It was in the middle of 1979 that the original Thompson Twins trio moved down to London and became a sextet. They made some records for some independent labels, and a bit of a reputation for themselves. The Thompson Twins' approach to music was somewhat *anthropological*. They were interested in African tribal rituals. They talked about 'spontaneity' and their look was studiedly bohemian; a jumble sale, dressed-down chic comprising baggy jumpers, grandaddy trousers and braces that needed buttons – not the nasty clip-on kind. Some of them also took to wearing little ribbons in their carefully unkempt hair to show respect for Third World culture. It was nothing like Boy George, but then he hadn't been invented yet.

The Twins also had certain counter-cultural political perspectives. They did 35 gigs on a No Nukes tour before CND had really got big again, and they would later refuse to share a billing with short-lived Bow Wow Wow copyists King Trigger because they considered their stage act to be sexist. Tom Bailey explained this, articulately, to the music press.

Indeed, there was a *theoretical* backdrop to most of the things the Thompson Twins did. One strand of punk-era anti-rock rhetoric concerned itself with the breaking down of barriers between performers and their audience. This often became corrupted into dozens of eager publicity-seekers leaping across the monitors for thirty seconds of instant fame. The Thompson Twins set themselves to turning the idea of the stage invasion into something more *meaningful*. Bits and pieces of disillusioned former actor Joe Leeway's percussive arsenal were handed out at gigs so that punters could join in properly (though they very often didn't give them back). In relation to all this stuff, Bailey contributed an article to the third edition of a Bristol-based magazine-and-record project called *Recorder*. The piece was entitled *The Participation Rap*, and, in it, Bailey explained how in Guinea entire communities took part in musical rituals 'lasting for many hours, even days – happy.'

The Twins had a song called *Politics* which, taking its cue from feminist thought, proposed that our every personal act is in truth political. They had another, called *Vendredi Saint*. This, broadly, was a chant, on which Leeway wailed in a lead voice which was his approximation of the African 'tribal' fashion.

Yes, it would not be unjust to say that the Thompson Twins were *those* sorts of

Behold, the international beatniks. Left to right: Leeway, Bailey and Currie.

people. Earnest, well-meaning, no doubt very genuinely concerned, but inclined to be a trifle tortuous about it. They probably liked to think that they weren't really engaging with the trashy, tacky mainstream of the worst of western life, and by 1981, before Rip Rig And Panic had led the passing phase for re-popularising the freer end of jazz and the novelty of Beatnik-speak, the Thompson Twins had become the first among the school of post-punk drop-outs.

How symbolic it is, then, of the complete demise of what used to be called the 'underground' that within two years the Thompson Twins – with a different line-up but not such very different ideas – would be emphatically *buying in*.

The story of the Thompson Twins' conversion is no more succinctly told than by the sleeve of their 1984 album, *Into The Gap* – the one that took them to the top.

It was a hugely successful record, selling over a million copies in the UK. Four out of its nine tracks ended up as domestic hit singles, and the Twins became the latest British group to go big time transatlantic.

What they did so cleverly was translate the Boho Way into the language of the high street. The idea of music as an international language had been central to their approach, so, with more than a little hard sales insight, they marketed themselves as *global*. There they are on the cover of *Into The Gap*, vaulting all the boundaries. Three globes; three little jet aircraft facsimiles zooming past. Bailey and Leeway alone remained from the old band, and they had recruited Alannah Currie, an itinerant New Zealander, to complete a trio. So here we had the perfect line-up: one black man, one white man and one woman – harmony of race and sex, unity of world. Game, set and mix and match.

The reverse side of the album's sleeve shows greater sophistication still. The new Twins had already done the proper presentation thing on their first album together, 1982's *Quick Step And Side Kick*. That is, they had created a mock-corporate monogram which could be maintained from product to product like a seal of established quality. In their case, the three heads were outlined, silhouetted, and coloured in where the hair would be. This recurs as you'd expect on the front of *Into The Gap*, but on the back the trio of head shapes are represented again as land masses on a world map, complete with lines of latitude and longitude. The track listing appears below, printed on a mock geological cross-section derived from the 'map' above. Design by Satori, art direction by Nick Marchant and Alannah. The message? Crystal clear. 'Cross-cultural' pop with all the trimmings.

It was like street theatre with business machines. As self-contained, self-employed entrepreneurs, the Thompson Twins were thoroughly proficient. They had all the ideas and most of the expertise. Alannah played percussion and oversaw the clothes, the artwork and the videos. Joe played keyboards and directed what turned out to be highly-polished hi-tech live shows. Tom sang, played all sorts of things, did most of the writing and generally acted as figurehead. Their music was perfectly groomed and accessible, both immediate and 'intelligent'. They had a reputation for working themselves stupid. Nothing was going to stop them.

There were those who accused the new Thompson Twins of selling out, but that was a silly attitude to take. All the Twins had done was move onto the shopping mall. What they were doing now was no more artificial than all that back-to-instinct-like-the-natives stuff, and considerably less pretentious. It may be a tribute to their essential shallowness, but the basic Twins philosophy was almost precisely the same. The music was still rhythmic, to-the-point, had 'ethnic' bits hanging off, and carried an enveloping sentiment which was no better or worse than that of *I'd Like To Teach The World To Sing*. The difference was that they were better *designed*.

Arista Records, a desperately unfashionable company throughout the reign of

Punk and just about everything since, sensed that they were on to a fat one, and they went for it. £200,000 was ploughed into the newly-favoured promotional channel, TV advertising. Arista claimed this to be 'the biggest ever TV support to a contemporary album'. Aside from the expected fly-posting and full-page magazine ads, elements of the sleeve's graphics were plastered all over shop fronts. It was claimed that more than 300,000 copies of the album had been ordered up in advance of its release. *Music Week* quoted Arista's managing director David Simone thus: 'the marketing budget for *Into The Gap*, reflects my belief that the Thompson Twins have tremendous staying power as a major act worldwide.' That's leisure capital – working hard at bringing people closer.

'Worldwide' was a vital idea in the Twins' great leap forward. Superficial cross-fertilisations of musical forms was all the rage and selling fast. All sorts of Latin American, Caribbean and West African titbits now decorated the creations of the big pop successes who'd streamed out of clubland and gone national, some international. The magpie approach was perfectly manageable for the Twins who'd been there before with different haircuts.

We might have expected an earlier Thompson Twins to have had moral qualms about all this. But suddenly there was no longer any contradiction between wanting to make 'universal, cross-cultural music' (Tom's words) and embracing the central mechanisms of Western capitalism. *Communication*, was what mattered in the end; reaching people. The Twins got stuck into every department of promotion. After all, Tom explained, if you were 'aimed *culturally* as an international group,' it was 'a natural side effect' to be involved in every aspect of shifting the product. So that was all right.

The key to the Thompsons' musical transformation was their discovery of electronic instruments. Synthesisers and drum machines enabled them to fulfil the now dominant demand for pop to be dance-floor competent. Hot, crisp, black dance music had always required razor-sharp playing; lean, economical, stretched tight. Now something approaching its exquisite tension could be put together on machines. *In The Name Of Love*, the first release from the new line-up, showed that they had got the hang of it. Everything important was there: synthetic chattering rhythm, synthetic bassline pulse, synthetic horn punctuations, synthetic Steve Lillywhite production. For *Quick Step And Side Kick* Compass Point house producer Alex Sadkin applied his own brand of silicon finish, not just to the bits of funk, but whatever else took the 'universally, cross-culturally' inclined threesome's fancy. Consequently the collection is littered with trans-global references as before, but now coated in the antiseptic hi-tech veneer which characterised a whole bunch of vogue LPs in the early '80s. (Compass Point became the country seat of cosmopolitan computer rhythms. Especially notable was Grace Jones' collaboration with reggae sessioneers Sly Dunbar and Robbie Shakespeare. Jones also contributes backing vocals to the *Quick Step* track, *Watching*.)

Thus, the *Quick Step* album has some neatly planned professional moments. *Lies*, with its reggae percussion, attractive lilt, and Chinese figures for novelty effect has a certain swaggering charm. *Love On Your Side* is a re-write off that first 45, actually referring back to it at one point. Yes, they were learning all right.

They got the hang of video too; and their rather stagey promos bear eloquent witness to pop's ever-increasing catchment area in the Post-punk era.

The Thompson Twins' videos are not the works of cheeky proles or chinless playboys. Rather they betray the visions of self-made squatters. It's play power theory practised on TV. The Twins tend to overact, as if demonstrating the importance of self-expression to junior school children. The charisma of Lennox, the rapaciousness of Frankie and the bitter-sweet comedy of Madness have made

'Don't you know it's gonna be. . .alright?'

their forays into the new front room medium like series of sharply executed coup de pop. They've transformed going public into a kind of disparate modern electronic theatre. The Thompson Twins, on the other hand, tended to be purely *theatrical*.

Listening to the track *Lies* we got the impression that there was something a bit keen and cryptic going on. The video undermined it. It was a Magritte-inspired pretend surrealist production and dreadfully *dressy*, with 'mystical' waving hands, and exaggerated gesticulations. For *Love On Your Side* they did better. It had a good director (Brian Grant) and a diverting set (bits of fawny fabric, rope, and shadows projected onto canvas), but the ham thespianisms still came ten-a-penny. The look draws, tellingly, on the naive tradition. Bailey appears with his clean white shirt buttoned to the top. His red henna'd hair is brushed strictly into a little boy fringe. Then there's Alannah: oversize cartoon curls, oversize Dr Martens, oversize railway engineer cap: baby girl urchin hasn't grown into her clothes yet! Add to this Leeway's emphatically high-fashion dreadlocks and we get the full picture of the Thompson Twins' image – sort of North London Sensitive, hemmed and stream-lined for the silicon age. It's a look which appears at its most mannered in their video for *We Are Detective*, probably the most *performed* of their promos. The song's 'continental' castanet touches and prim tango dance-step are played out in the most literal fashion. Taking the detective theme at face value, they play at being Bogart and Bacall in an uncomfortable piece of repertory which really showed their age: middle twenties to thirties parading themselves as innocents.

The faking of innocence is a central idea in the 'new pop' but those who've played on it best have utilised the trimmings of naivety to delight in how *knowing* they are. They handle themselves in such a way as to let us see the pretence at work. The Twins, though, really do like us to believe that they are still unspoiled by vulgarity and greed, rebuffing all suggestions that they are, even in the narrowest respect, just another piece of product.

For instance, they really like America a lot 'but not for the reason most people do.' Most people like it 'because it reminds them of TV.' But the TTs are a little above all that. 'As a pop group with international aims, as it were,' Tom explained; 'it is particularly fascinating because it is like a scaled down version of the world. You haven't got just one culture there. You've not only got black and white, male and female, but you've also got Puerto Rican immigrants, Mexican immigrants and a lot of European culture as well.' Nothing transient and disposable about the people who are named after the detectives in Hergé's *Adventures of Tintin*. They are, remember, 'aimed *culturally* as an international group.' They don't make music, 'just for the people around us.' Oh no. 'We make music for the whole planet.'

The most refreshing thing about the 'new pop' was that it acknowledged its limitations, and this realism was the flipside of its vanity. By constant reference to pulp's past it was almost as if it was examining itself. There was grit within the candyfloss, an understanding that little could be less sincere than cosmetic culture trying to be 'good for us'.

The Thompson Twins, though, continue to try their best. But what does it amount to? Here's a quote from Alannah, reproduced on Arista's press release for review copies of *Into The Gap*: 'we wanted to touch what is "human" and common to all people, regardless of age, sex or race. Rhythm was our starting point because it has that driving heart-beat. Everyone has a heart.' A glossy foldout which came inside the record continued this tender touching of our human parts. The page devoted to Thompson Twins merchandise addresses us as *individuals*. 'This is to introduce you to our Fan Club,' goes the blurb; 'it is run by friends of ours who will try to give you a service which is as personal as possible.' To the peoples of the world, the Thompson Twins made available the following: four differently designed T-shirts; two sets of button badges; the 1984 Tour Programme (swiftly out of date at £2.60); a baseball cap; a satin pennant; six full colour postcards; a ten inch by two foot nylon flag with inverted 'V' for £4.25. All prices payable by cheque or postal order, cashed, one presumes, with a caring personal touch.

The almost farcical efforts by the Twins try to persuade us that they are a bit more significant than the rest of the common flotsam is what causes them to be rather less. They neither wrestle with the contradictions nor accept them. Rather, they pretend they are not there. As a result, the only bridges built, 'culturally' or otherwise, are between pre-teens (who buy their singles) and student types (who buy the albums). Into The Gap? Into the *market* gap, more like.

As such, the 'message' of the Twins is an entirely facile one. It aspires to finer things, but is so devoid of political nouse and the humility which admits doubt, that it radiates little more than fatuous postures and empty liberal gestures. These tell us nothing about the ways of the world on the one hand, or the ways of pop on the other. Almost all of *Into The Gap* relies on euphoric crescendos and over-dramatic laments which do little justice to otherwise perfectly reasonable themes of spiritual liberation (*You Take Me Up*), sexual liberation (*Sister Of Mercy*) or liberating love

(*Hold Me Now*, *Doctor Doctor*). Like the videos which helped to sell them they are not so much cathartic as overwrought.

This face-pulling front conceals a complacency which is typical of the relics of that crumbling early '70s counter culture, one which has either capitulated to marginalised sentimentality (street theatre) or become spoiled overgrown schoolboy bastions of hip leisure capitalism (Virgin Emperor Richard Branson, or Tony Elliot, publisher of exhausted, geriatric *Time Out* magazine, once described by a very well known design person as 'Like an old man in a pink suit').

That the Twins represent the ways of the last underground generation is neatly illustrated by their cover version of the Beatles' *Revolution* on the 1985 album *Here's To Future Days*. 'Don't you know it's gonna be alright!,' John Lennon had screamed in 1968 and may have meant it, only to spend years after the Fab Four – who broke down a few consumer divisions themselves – finally fell out trying to tell us that it wasn't. *Here's To Future Days* said you don't need drugs and you don't need guns – all you need is love. Here was ethnicised anti-materialism gone dayglo. The last segment of the market had been coloured in and gift-wrapped. Yesterday's wholemeal platitude had become today's fast food treat – in a sesame seed bun.

12

ELVIS COSTELLO
Pretty Words Don't Mean Much Anymore

Elvis Costello had a problem. He was too good at the game to be asked on to the team. It was a losing battle which was probably not worth winning, though he fought it hard for years. The trouble was, no-one wanted to hear the bad news anymore, and Elvis told it very, very well. Melancholic, witty, intuitive and caustic, Elvis loved a pretty lie; and what Elvis liked to do was turn those pretty lies so bitter-sweetly upside down.

From the word go it was Costello and no other who led the field in grafting Punk's half-crazed disdain onto the traditional pop disciplines of melody, symmetry and lyrical panache. With *My Aim Is True*, his debut album of 1977, he showcased a rare, poisonous and passionate talent bursting to be heard. He had good tunes, an abrasive voice and a bunch of crisply crafted lyrics, jammed with hurt. But what really made him different was that he knew about the past.

Although he was only 22, Costello's compositions drew on just as many years of transatlantic pop and R&B constructions. He betrayed himself as a connoisseur of his art's rich heritage and chose not to blast yesterday into smithereens but to customise it. He tuned it into the wavelength of the modern world. Costello made plagiarism creative, wrenching the sound of British pub rock from its time warp, reviving the resonance of the three-minute pop song, and made the dead end language of Punk *really* start to talk.

Costello is the first classicist of ephemera. Rather than worship disposability for its own sake, his early output picked up on those conventions and used them to take revenge on a world in love with pulp. *Watching The Detectives*, which became his first top twenty single in 1978, brilliantly crystalised a deep distaste for fakery. Also the first Costello track to feature the Attractions, *Detectives* had the singer observing grisly proceedings from both sides of the TV set, sneering at both the entertainers and the entertained with the revolted fascination of a schoolboy dismembering a butterfly. The record's terse, punk reading of reggae cut across an eerie guitar line recalled the theme to the seedy ITV series *Callan*, espionage drama's first antidote to the cosmetic glamour of Bond. *Detectives* made for traumatic listening. It announced Costello's arrival as pop's final solution to the false optimism that had given it life.

His fervour was quite murderous. Nothing on the first three albums offered much light at the end of what he seemed to perceive as a labyrinth of tunnels choked up with stupidity and fear. *My Aim Is True*, *This Year's Model* (1978) and *Armed Forces*

Elvis: downbeat musicologist. Pictured by Peter Anderson.

(1979) together comprise a trilogy of exhilarated malice. Each built logically on the one before it, broadening its perspective, refining its tradecraft, and with each progression the artist's prestige and popularity rose.

Aim's jokey sleeve concept played on a comic contrast between gawky, horn-rimmed Costello and the *other* Elvis. This pinpoints nicely the quest and the context of the 'new wave' anti-star. Presley had been deemed love's universal conqueror, the one who made it all easy, who opened up a million possibilities. More than twenty years later, Costello jibed that legend by making rock a vehicle for total romantic failure. He became characterised as Mr Guilt and Vengeance, seemingly directing his venom at every girl who'd ever jilted him, and it sounded like there'd been a few of those. Some labelled him misogynist. But true misogynists don't think about it that much. And, anyway, Costello's brief was wider than that. He was as much a stylist as a confessor. His fight was with the great clichés of passion, and by twisting them inside out he wrought a ruthless evocation of perpetual disaster. Untainted tenderness surfaced only once, on the ballad *Alison*, which nonetheless contained the adamant declaration that *he* wasn't going to get too sentimental. He needn't have worried. We'd already got the point.

Pop culture's saccharined fallacy was that the cushiest thing in life was to be young and in love. Costello set about re-writing history. *This Year's Model* was the first album he made with the Attractions (*Aim* had been played by Clover, a session band). Bruce Thomas (bass), Pete Thomas (drums) and Steve Neive (keyboards) were all accomplished players who precisely captured the spirit of the proceedings from the off. Together, they harnessed Costello's pirated '60s signatures into the disillusioned present. *Model* systematically trashed the citadel of glamour, dragging up a range of false gods from a lost era of promised plenty, and crucifying the lot.

Where his purer Punk contemporaries saw rock/pop culture's yesteryears as times of risible blind idealism (the Pistols) or a corrupted culture which youth always should have rightly ruled (the Jam, Generation X) Costello saw the swinging years as the birthplace of a vapid consumerism whose failure had to be exposed. His malignancy was utterly modern, but the element of throwback was what gave it teeth. *Lipstick Vogue, (I Don't Want To Go To) Chelsea,* and *This Year's Girl* form the core of a collection to make the King's Road crumble with shame. Lyrics flickered with the minutiae of the beauty business. It wasn't a matter of pulling model girls' hair, more a desecration of showroom dummies. Costello delighted in finding cheap truths behind the glossy centrefold, with Neive's tinny Farfisa organ sound acting as a lovingly pre-fabricated counterpoint. Behind the smiling faces, Elvis sited nasty little minds.

Model is a kind of metaphor for twenty years of decline in which eyes were casually averted from imminent disaster. Both the first two albums contain nightmare visions of capitulation to fascism. *Less Than Zero* and *Night Rallies* are vehement, fearful attacks on the National Front, which at that time was a force which threatened to become significant. Then, with *Armed Forces*, we got the complete analysis.

This album was the brimming consummation of Costello's rise to unlikely stardom. The artist here was a triumphant absurdist, a man who saw everything too clearly for its hatefulness to damage his bubbling confidence. On *My Aim Is True*, Costello had come across as a walking catastrophe. *This Year's Model* indicated instead a sulphurous investigator with a switchblade mind and a chip on his shoulder – like the sleeve implied, an intruder behind the lens. But *Armed Forces* dealt in smooth, confident, sardonic absolutes.

Producer Nick Lowe's finish was a parody of hi-tech. The images of clean, ordered consumer comfort on the sleeve illustrated one half of a seemingly effortless exploration of what divided the comfortable classes from the beckoning social decline. The inviting tunes and crisp, graphic textures suggested the friendliest album yet, while its words mockingly, ironically, picked apart a tapestry of encroaching paranoia. The predominant mood of jingoistic reaction which would corral the British spirit in the years to come was sharply anticipated in the grooves and also by the original title which distributors WEA would not allow – 'Emotional Fascism'. It was an album of cool and cutting deceptions, complete enough on the track *Oliver's Army* – a systematic hymn of loathing to the related menaces of unemployment and militarism – to allow it to cruise unmolested to number two in the UK singles chart.

Oliver's Army clinched Elvis Costello's rise and, in the classic fashion of pop, marked the beginning of his fall. From self-pitying uglybug offering vicarious gratification to that part of everyone which often feels the same, Costello was now estimated as the smartest troubadour of the contemporary malaise. He had set himself apart from the rest of the school of '77, who by this time had either disintegrated or found it impossible to maintain a momentum based almost exclusively on white hot dismissive rhetoric.

Costello was a sophisticate of despair, whose song-writing flair enabled him to sustain. But with his flowering came a reputation for hatefulness. At first his feisty, vindictive persona amplified his appeal, and his bitterness was crucial to the pull of his public display. But the sentiments spoofed on the cover of *Aim* were suddenly leaping right off the cardboard and coming alarmingly to life. Costello cut himself off from the press and handed his audiences monosyllabic malice. There was a time when to attend one of his concerts was to become part witness, part object of abuse. His verdant distaste could be spellbinding. All in all, Elvis Costello possessed the morbid, yet poetic, attraction of a choreographed car crash.

But it was now his turn to become quite literally accident-prone, and the records which follow fascinate as the output – imagined or otherwise – of a champion pug taking too much punishment and coping with convalescence. As *Armed Forces* cracked America he appeared to have it made. Instead he suffered a series of serious batterings. During a major US tour, the infamous 'racist' incident occurred when Costello, apparently enraged by the sanctimony of a bunch of faded LA flower power perennials, was said to have resorted to a low kind of abuse in order to cause the greatest possible offence. In the States, where his proven record of anti-racist activism wasn't known about, his reputation has only recently recovered. Back home, legal problems beset his record company Radar. There were reports of a marital break-up. Relations with the music papers worsened to such an extent that stray reporters put themselves at physical risk if they approached. 'At the end of the *Armed Forces* period,' Costello would explain later to *New Musical Express*, 'I felt completely disillusioned with the idea of making records.'

Meanwhile, the musical tide was turning, and new currents prepared to make the play. There was a fresh embrace of traditional pop values which, in a way, logically reflected the sense of futility which Punk had sought to express. After all, where else was there to go? Costello had pilfered pop classicism to add clout to his commentary on the present day. He was pop culture's most educated undertaker. The new breed robbed the grave.

Barely had the polemic of anti-stardom died away when the pursuit of acquiescent celebrity status became acceptable again. In London, the pub gave way to the club as the breeding ground for new signings, new faces, and a new cult of mystique and exclusivity. The race was overtly on again for the good things in life, as invective went out of style. The self-publicists of recessionary ragtime rose from the underworld to claim the spotlight. They smiled for the camera. They wanted to be cool, detached, desirable, aloof. Their music was borrowed without respect, their look, irreverently eclectic, their aspirations sheer Babylonian Hollywood – nostalgia is the opium of the slump.

Till now, Elvis Costello had seemed exhilarated by the force of his own displeasure. But in the new decade, music's ways and means reversed into a more pliant form of media role-playing, and his abrasion became steadily consigned to the margins. The changing mood coincided with the songwriter's most depressed record yet.

For all its superficial levity, *Get Happy* (1980) is dense, neurotic and crawling with horrors. It was easy to miss the point. To start with *Get Happy* contained no less than twenty tracks, each a quick-fire picture postcard portrait. As the spoof '60s artwork indicates, both the musical benchmarks and its format are intended as a tribute to the Motown and Stax schools of soul, of which Costello remains an ardent admirer. Nick Lowe's flawlessly mock-mono, bottom-heavy production adds to the superficial impression of fun. But closer inspection reveals almost unbroken grimness. This was the sound of the song machine gone almost out of control. Ostensibly a record reliant on an in-joke and a groove, its wordplay lies in wait, a punishing punch in the mouth.

Lines are constructed like collages of advertising puns and couplets, or little cascades of newspaper captions. The effect is like a battery of bad-news banner headlines. The semantics are deliberately throwaway, their flippancy mocking the scenarios they describe. Costello's language brilliantly apes the callous truth behind the glibness of mainstream mediaspeak. As usual, he is besotted with the bits and pieces of pulp, and, while the rest of the world went hi-tech, Elvis Costello went monochrome downbeat, drawing on a succession of clinching metaphors for give-away givingness.

There is little hint of smart-alecry or gleeful self-satisfaction in the delivery of his obsessively juggled conceits. They are spat out like third hand gum. *Get Happy* is riddled with picaresque glimpses of tattered romance and soiled passion. All the perfume is cheap: 'Those days she was just a beautiful girl, now she's framed and hung up.' (*Black And White World*). It should all be a back slap, a bunch of party pieces, but it doesn't come across like that. The feeling is more one of give 'em what they want till they choke. *Get Happy* comes loaded with the trimmings of a recent time when there was no room for doubt, while its contents mimic that same time's degenerating fabric. Costello's singing became as tortured as it's ever got. On *Hi Fidelity* and *Riot Act*, he sounds like a man in his death throes. As gags go, *Get Happy* was a very bitter crack.

The album's trailer single, a cover of a Sam And Dave 'B'-side called *I Can't Stand Up For Falling Down*, reintroduced Costello to the British public, and went to number four. But *Get Happy*, the first album to be released on the new F-Beat label, was a commercial failure. So clustered a package did not attract pure pop punters, nor did it satisfy those anticipating an endorsement of more obviously political alignments. It was not a chummy little item at all. Subsequent singles *Hi Fidelity* and *New Amsterdam* (a waltz tune in revolt against New York chic) also failed to get the cash registers singing. It was clear that Costello was a victim of both the tendencies he'd so furiously attacked, and the ones he'd helped to start. His stylisations had been a critique of pop's fatuousness. The new pop beauties soon came merely to glory in it.

The LP which followed, *Trust* (1981), seemed like an admission of commercial rejection. As pop went in search of the total packaging concept, this was an album which almost perversely decided to be eclectic, difficult, eccentric. In smart new

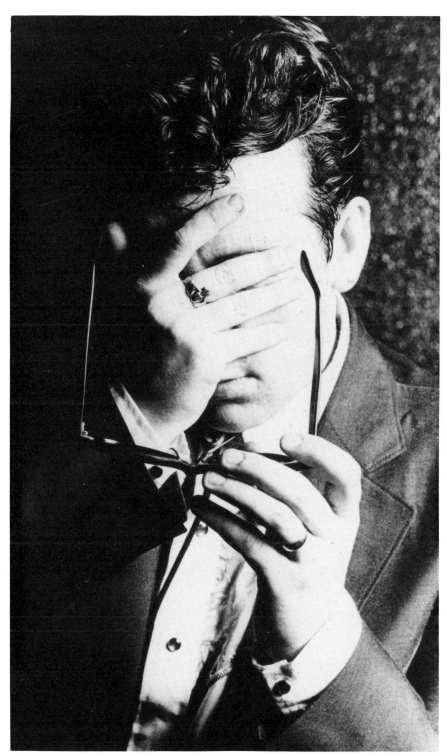

'And I would rather be anywhere else than here today'. Elvis photographed by Anton Corbijn.

111

magazines a jerry built mythology was being constructed around the London club scene and becoming the focus of everyone's attention. On *Clubland* Costello derides nocturnal pleasure fetishism as the pastime of the facile and devious. As the imagery or narcissism lost its nerve and headed upmarket in anticipation of the millions to come, Elvis surrounded himself jokily with the down at heel fixtures of '40s film noir. The sleeve photos see the band set up among accoutrements of the jazz age, but they are grimy and worn; not at all like Kid Creole. The artist himself is pictured as something that escaped from the pages of Raymond Chandler. The front cover shot simply celebrates a matured but basically unaltered image; jacket, collar, tight little tie, threatened widow's peak – glasses that were groovy in Buddy Holly's day. There is a flicker of humour in the mouth and eyes. It is the perfect sleeve for a record which matches a low-key sense of parody, and an established, hard boiled way with words. The artwork's innuendo, deliberate or not, was that the Costello approach was now too refined and too adult to be welcome in the limelight, and in the track *Pretty Words* he confirmed it. It wasn't really what the new pop public wanted to hear.

Trust seems like a record in half-resigned revolt against the grand Top Forty gallop which started as a glowing pleasure, but swiftly declined into bloated vacuity. The vogue tendency was to deal in big, bold spectacle and promote yourself as the star, but Costello became more and more beguiled by the secret world of detail. *Trust* was a piece of pop reportage rather than actual chart-topping pop itself. Its content ranged over every field of popular songwriting that took its maker's eye. *Different Finger* is a straight excursion into the adultery tradition of country and western. *Lovers Walk* revamps the Bo Diddley riff to retitle the famous walkway Muggers Alley. *Strict Time* turns on a pretend formality filched from *Classical Gas* and spells out a pulverising socialite put-down. Various ballad traditions are called on as well as Swing, and, in *From a Whisper To A Scream* the more familiar stomp of vintage soul, where Squeeze's Glen Tilbrook contributes a euphoric share of the vocal. The song seemed tailored for the chart – but it never came to be.

Easy handholds were in short supply on *Trust* and its fragmentary format made it an album for the preacher and his flock above all. It's an ornate, strictly *investigative* collection, a melancholic step into songwriting traditions which have survived the march of time. And when it was decided to go to Nashville and record a full-blown country album with bad-tempered production legend Billy Sherrill, it amounted to an implicit acknowledgement of exclusion from the great pop game.

There was no other option by this time. Costello's career had been driven by a critique. He'd wanted to murder the mythology of pop through a fervent kind of scorched earth satire. But the first rule of parody is to watch out for reality – it tends to blunder in. So Costello became marginalised by parasites on his own imagination. The new breed didn't want to sweep the past away; they wanted to revive it as eternal, equivocating camp.

It wasn't just the introduction of a spoof look and '60s licks which set the rock industry to plundering its own treasure trove. The entire presentation of Costello encouraged the embrace of nostalgia as a springboard for ongoing rock industry expediency. His career had commenced with Stiff Records, the initially humble project of former Dr Feelgood road manager Andrew Jakeman, popularly known as Jake Riviera. The Stiff operation was poor, irreverant, witty and firmly rooted in pub rock, about the only indigenous genre worth bothering with in the barren middle '70s. Riviera put together a stable of artists, most of whom were talented survivors of the 'rhythm and booze' set. Costello (real name Declan MacManus) was a computer operator and unsung undergraduate of the circuit. He'd had previous experience in folk clubs (sharp-tongued singer-songwriter) and in a reportedly undistinguished country blues outfit called Flip City.

Under the assumed name DP Costello (the surname was his mother's maiden name) our man was the first to respond to Riviera's advertisement for material from unsigned acts. He submitted an impressive cassette of songs which formed the basis of *My Aim Is True*. Christening MacManus after 'the other Elvis' was, apparently, Riviera's idea.

This was the first step in what became Stiff's greatest gift; tarting up what might otherwise have been prematurely dismissed as secondhand goods. Thus Ian Dury, Nick Lowe, Larry Wallis and Wreckless Eric re-appeared as colourful streetwise vagabonds with titillating tales to tell. Stiff pillaged forgotten conventions to put the razzle back into marketing. They resuscitated picture sleeves and a distinctive label logo. Their press advertisements and hoardings used off-the-wall 'personality' tactics and brilliantly oblique slogans to create both artist and company identity. It all helped cultivate a knock on sales effect: If It Aint Stiff It Aint Worth A Fuck, etcetera. Stiff became a family outfit serviced by committed devotees who religiously purchased every release. The acts toured as a package — A Bunch of Stiffs – something not seen since the Stax/Volt soul revues of some fifteen years before.

Stiff's tactics, like Elvis Costello's songs, were cryptic and aggressive. But their achievements as field leaders of the then booming independent label sector was swiftly pirated by the majors who, predictably, replaced the originators' shoestring cheek with opulent emptiness. A glut of revivalism – remember 'Power Pop'? – eventually settled into a more subtle, more catholic kind of plagiarism. Enter the reign of subliminal re-processed packaging.

The pretty new things gleamed from the small screen and the pages of *Smash Hits*. Video advanced upon the peoples of the world, only rarely to useful effect. So, the writer was eclipsed by the signifier, the commentator by the self-publicist, the artist by the designer. Pop clamours to be part of the general racket of media and merchandise once again, placing itself firmly and unapologetically into the foreground of shiny commerce, not as an irritant, but as a willing and ready collaborator. Now past thirty and well past a sales peak which he hit with *Armed Forces* in 1979, Elvis Costello is, in some ways, fortunate to still be functioning as a major act. Within a couple of years his circumstances had changed drastically enough to relegate him from contender for some imaginary post-punk throne and turn him into the essentially minority interest he is now.

Perhaps Costello's search since *Get Happy* had been for something with which to replace his initial concentrated rage. 'I just got tired of it,' he told the *NME*, 'also, you become a bit pathetic after a while if you're still ranting on.' Since his exclusion from the immediate foreground, he found himself in a curious territory, hovering somewhere between eternal stateliness and being a beleaguered victim of circumstance. Musically he roamed productively enough into the furthest corners of his wide-ranging interests; to country with *Almost Blue* which worked well as a showcase for his voice, and what, by his own admission, was a profound sense of desolation; and also deeper into southern soul, with several of the tracks on 1983's *Punch The Clock* where the TKO Horns and backing singers Afrodiziak added mass to the Attractions basic sound.

When you look at those two albums, at '84s uneven *Goodbye Cruel World* and '82s bizarrely brilliant *Imperial Bedroom*, what strikes is not any particular endemic lack of inspiration, but a certain absence of *obviousness*. Things were simpler in the past – it always felt like the snotty guy in glasses was out to get something, someone, maybe even you. There was the compulsive vicarious excitement of watching the outsider bursting in to burn the playhouse to the ground. Elvis was straight and true, and going for the kill.

What came to stymie him was the way the pop market so wilfully excludes wisdom and complexity. The first revelatory collagist of the new pop phase, Costello became frustrated by comprehending its mechanisms far too well. The channelled venom and erudite disdain with which he delivered his bruising bulletins gave him his fame, but fiscally contained its own full stop.

He has aged, and so have his audience, many of whom, as pop consumers do, will have gone on to buying other things. A fresh generation, seemingly immunised against pop's more dangerous possibilities by relentless exposure to recessionary pragmatism, sought their reflections in other stars who took the traditional terms of pop as given, and played the game to win. Their message: the product, not its purpose, was the thing.

By contrast, Costello's output demanded an increasing appreciation of the finer points. His lyrics turned towards metaphors and nuances which are ever more subtle and ornate. The same might be said of his tunes. *Imperial Bedroom* was a collection truly worthy of a sharp talking sniper who'd burst the limitations of spite. Deftly, it picks through love-hate songs of real compassion and insight; tales of personal experience and unsettling observation. Edgy, off-the-wall and vaguely incomplete, it is the riskiest, most consistently engrossing of all his LPs. It is also his most reflective; and this settling of his formerly wounded ire made possible also breathless shards of social analysis like the shady, eerie *Pills and Soap*, and *Shipbuilding*, a co-composition with *Punch The Clock* producer Clive Langer which was first of all an impossibly plaintive hit for Robert Wyatt. An eloquent expression of the same connections explored in *Oliver's Army* it was written in protest against Britain's engagement in the Falklands War, and stands as the finest piece of political songwriting this decade. What a bitter irony then that facile pundits of the designer decade should be able to condemn so acute and radical a figure as a *Man Out Of Time*.

Civilised minds, it seems, are most at risk when blinkered certainties hold sway. And with the odds stacked against him, 'Elvis Costello' – a switchblade allegory blunted by its own expertise – was consigned to a place in history by his creator in the early months of 1986. Declan MacManus – apparently a real person – stepped out of Elvis's skin, and made a record, *King of America*, which broke figuratively, if not quite literally, with his alter ego's past. Elvis Costello is dead; but the malady he mooted lingers on, an enduring reminder that the hunter in the great pop chase is fated to be captured by the game.

13

::

THE HUMAN LEAGUE
Everything With Chips

When *Don't You Want Me* went to number one at the tail of '81, it was hard to imagine a target hit more perfectly spot on. What a deliciously crafted fraud it was. The only genuine thing about it was its embrace of artifice. The only original thing about it was its artful re-conditioning of a dozen popular cultural clichés. The only natural thing about it was the seeming, seamless ease with which the pre-fabrication was accomplished.

What we had here was a highly stylised romantic stereotype. Wounded Philip Oakey and wounding Susanne Sulley related both sides of a terminating love match. Philip insisted he had taken her from obscurity to fame, and now she said she didn't need him any more. Susanne maintained that this had been his choice, and why should it put her under some eternal obligation anyway? Oakey's voice was a mannered baritone. Susanne's, aching earnestly, snook out faintly flat. The backing track was synthesised and produced with immaculate clarity. Melodically the song was strong and packed with pathos. A firmly pulsing backbeat underlined the whole. How simply *exquisite* it was.

Don't You Want Me's chart-topping reign became as memorable visually as musically, thanks to Steve Barron's video. As the song hinted at self-mockery, so Barron's promo neatly unravelled its narrative strands and built into them whole new dimensions of insincerity, highlighting still further the utterly fictitious innocence of the thing. Until then, few videos had attempted to do much more than simply showcase their subjects, or, at best, provide a screenplay of the most literal kind. But Barron's effort did much, much more. What it actually is is a video of the making of a make-believe movie, whose plot is a love affair based on supermarket pulp, derived from a pop song, and made to be shown on TV; layer upon layer upon layer of myth-making media gift-wrap.

It drew from a huge range of sources: film noir, pre-war matinee deities, Mills and Boon, soap-operatics, science fiction, Raymond Chandler, Hollywood Babylonia, James Bond and a whole unwritten catalogue of modernist mannerisms. The entire *Don't You Want Me* campaign was a flawlessly executed exercise in objectified desirability, and its shameless self-consciousness in relation to all this was the key to its considerable charm.

With *Don't You Want Me*, the Human League confirmed their rise as a different and most efficacious pop force. Here was a group which had formed originally as a quartet of male non-musicians who believed pop, as a conspiracy of sound and

From underground spaceman to overground Starman – the Philip Oakey transformation.

117

vision, could be constructed with machines. They were experimental, underground fringe-Punk weirdos, who David Bowie went to see. Now, suddenly, a rather different Human League were everybody's pin-ups, from *My Guy* to *Smash Hits*, to *The Face*, to the *Daily Star*. And yet, the principles were pretty much the same.

The new Human League at once fed an urge for novelty and for nostalgia. Their newness lay in their sound, the first breakout of pure synthesiser music from the rarefied field of boffinism, art or continental disco. This, they applied to boy-versus-girl scenarios of the classic kind, complete with text book tunes, chorus, beat and hooks. Not that they limited themselves to the back issues of pop *music*. No, their pillaging extended to the entire directory of post-war disposability and beyond: trashy novels, low rent movies, cheapo fashions, tawdry symbols of glamour. It was as if within the Human League a whole fragmented history of throwaway consumerism was enshrined.

Glibly, the League were shunted in amongst the precious front-runners of the new romance, but they served as excellent examples of everything about that 'movement' which was not new at all. The only different thing about the Human League was how they put themselves together – they were a pop phenomenon in kit form.

The original Human League came together in Sheffield in 1977. Though they swiftly came to be characterised as austere, rather pompous eggheads with very few human feelings to share, the impression made by their early work, interviews and live performances was of terminal adolescents working hard at keeping adulthood at bay. In their favour was what we might charitably describe as a sense of their own absurdity. This manifested itself in Philip Oakey's preposterous haircut (shoulder length on one side, short on the other), and the slide shows compiled by Adrian Wright (who did not play an instrument or sing) to accompany the quartet when they stepped out on stage – outings notable for the fact that you could scarcely see Wright or synthesists Martyn Ware and Ian Craig-Marsh at all. Also, for the way that Philip barely twitched an eyebrow throughout. They were, in short, ridiculous, and their greatest asset was that they appeared to appreciate the fact.

The Human League's quest, though, was serious. They strove not for rock'n'roll (their rather fetching version of the Gary Glitter song was there to prove it) but for an arena in which they could communicate carefully considered *ideas*. Music was one part of this, images another. They made their noise with things which could be operated with very little instrumental technique, and with tapes which they could create beforehand. Wright's dual projectors provided a string of science-fictional and auto-suggestive 'future tech' pictures. Characters from *Star Trek* were particular favourites, which was appropriate enough, since Oakey's delivery of looping tunes like *Empire State Human* and *Being Boiled* reminded you of the halting speech employed by the series' characters: imagine Mr Spock in the throes of existential angst.

Live, the result was a true multi-media occasion, a celebration of non-biodegradable culture conducted straight-faced, but with a delicate irony and a faint glimmer of Glam. There was no spontaneity about a Human League performance. With them, the stage was a shopfront, and they were the dummies. Rock'n'roll had been about losing control. The Human League were about achieving it. The received understanding of rock'n'roll's cycle was that what started out wild and exciting gradually became absorbed by the establishment, and tamed. The new pop stars broke the loop. Pop became a matter for study, a concept for grown-ups to investigate, and anyone from five to forty-five to consume. From the beginning, the Human League were the blueprint for a product awaiting development. Their manager Bob Last, also the founder of a company called Fast Product, was exactly the kind of business maverick they needed to put them together. Last would explain eloquently why, even for intellectuals, the days of going underground had gone. The trick now was to elbow your way in. 'You live in a world of product. I may not like the present situation, but if you want to do anything positive, you've got to accept certain things about it and work on its terms. I don't believe in dropping out, or alternative culture or any of this nonsense. You've got to get in there and struggle.'

With his records and his 'packages' (one Fast Product was a plastic bag with bits of 'debris' in it), Last applied provocations devised for theatre audiences by Bertholt Brecht to the detritus of western consumerism. Pop records were both a useful example of, and a vehicle for, this, and the Human League fitted perfectly into the Fast equation. Together they embarked on copying, parodying and revelling in standard entertainment practices, not so much with the idea of beating them at their own game as making the game more fun.

The new Human League was the very logical consequence of all this. After a pair of deeply unsuccessful albums for Virgin – *Reproduction* and *Travelogue* – Ware and Marsh departed amidst much bickering to form Heaven 17 with Glenn Gregory, where they created a kind of credit card socialist disco manifesto and became phenomenally hip for a very short time.

Oakey and Wright, meanwhile, made certain adjustments to their looks and aspirations and threw themselves into the deep end of the mainstream. As Oakey told *NME* in 1980, shortly before the dissolution of the original group, 'to me, a live show is what you do because you can't get on TV.' The new line-up steered itself irresistibly in front of the cameras. Avant-gardeist tendencies withered away, and as Heaven 17 headed for a theoretical dancefloor, Oakey and Wright headed for the eyeliner and theoretical heartstrings.

The resultant album, *Dare*, was the first masterpiece of revised pop priorities. It was pure *design*. In it, the group bridged the old, oversimplified credibility gap in white music wherein Pop had been associated with manufactured starlets with large smiles and small brains, and Rock with genuine, self-directed thinking *artists*. The Human League did the thinking for themselves. They took on the trappings and symbols of spangled glamour as part of their vocabulary. *Dare*'s cover was a direct parody of *Vogue* magazine, fashion publishing's crème de la crème. Rock logic had always decried fashion as a facile distraction from the business of making 'real' music. The Human League knew that it had nourished music's commercial survival and populist appeal.

There were certain crucial line-up changes. Joanne Catherall and Susanne Sulley were recruited as backing singers and stage dancers, a complement to Oakey in the vital creation of a chemistry of romance. Even the story of their discovery – schoolgirls wrenched from home and futurist disco to become overnight celebs – fuelled the sexual intrigue provoked by the sight of one man accompanied by two younger girls.

In the panic following Ware and Craig-Marsh's departure, Wright had taken a crash course in synth-playing, and the group's strength was augmented by local bass-player Ian Burden and later by experienced 'new wave' guitarist Jo Callis. These were the first conventional musicians to contribute to the Human League, and Callis added an extra sophistication to the compositional side. Neither, though, played guitars on *Dare*, where everything was made with chips. Producer Martin Rushent applied the final, pristine, textural finish to a supremely alluring pop commodity of many painstakingly perfect parts.

Last, Rushent and the League took the ground rules of pop classicism and made them work as well as anyone. *Dare*'s contents won over every appropriate corner of

Human League being famous, circa '81.

an increasingly disparate record-buying public. It was danceable, so it could be played in white dance clubs. Emminently commercial, it fitted easily on to radio playlists. Resplendent in its studio polish, it highlighted the qualities of ever more elaborate domestic stereo systems. Further, *Dare* worked both as an album and as a breeding ground for singles. No less than four of its eight tracks would eventually see the light as successful 45s. As the cash registers rattled, and the press gang thundered over the hills, the Human League united the nation with their hip MOR manoeuvres, conducted with tongues *just about* in their cheeks – or so some of us liked to think.

As their noise was tailored for all occasions, so their style lent itself to every channel of promotion. Oakey, now rid of his bizarre coiffure, became gelled into an acceptable pin-up. The girls looked their Top Shop best. Harnessed together, the threesome were something beguiling and unique. *Don't You Want Me?* and the previous single *Love Action*, virtually translated themselves into video visuals. The *Love Action* promo cross-cut a glut of the League's adolescent daydreams with a collage of trash TV innuendos. A tormented Oakey looks on at a wedding. Domestic strife ensues in a hard-to-let tenement block, all broken and boarded up like a bombsite. Adrian combines two favourite roles, as technical whizz kid and as secret agent, monitoring the protagonists' every move in this Carry On With Cupid production. At the promo's close, a copy of the *Dare* album (for which *Love Action* was the trailer) appears dappled with confetti. A parody of a plug in a campaign to sell the more profitable long-player. Well, why pretend?

These efforts took the video into important new territory. A previous clip, accompanying *Open Your Heart*, had been shot entirely in a studio, which hardly helped to dispel that indefinable 'hardness' which can occur with video tape. Primitive computer graphics only added to this sense of the low rent, which wasn't in the spirit of the thing at all. From now on, video had to be *epic*. The League's chart domination at the end of '81 ushered in a period in which not only would pop promos be crucial parts of pop commerce, but organically united with the records and the public personas of the stars. Without a video it would now be next to impossible to have a major hit, and without at least twenty grand it would be difficult to make the right kind of video at all. The Human League, from being the bit part players of post-punk, were suddenly the Rolls Royce of Born Again pop.

Dare declared itself a luxury item for mass consumption. Oakey and the girls, the record's svelte, gatefold sleeve, and Rushent's wipe clean finish all conspired in the product's air of being a hygienic, desirable object, a tasteful thing to have around. The sounds and the songs, in a very *deliberate* way, declared an intention to embark upon the more attractive options life seemed to offer: love, travel, enjoyment for its own sake. In this context, even the forbidding *Seconds* (inspired, Oakey said, by the assassination of John F. Kennedy – Mr Glamour Power himself) and *I Am The Law* (a nightmare of a future police state along the lines of *2,000 AD*) simply became textural pre-requisites for a soapy epic which rummaged through the dustbin entertainment of the previous forty years and turned it all into conveyor-belt melodrama. They even opened side two with the theme from Michael Caine's 1971 thriller *Get Carter* – as if to prove the point.

But what made it all so cute was the group's contrasting qualities of irony and ordinariness. Whether by accident or design, Oakey's mannered monotone always suggested laughter behind the earnest mask. Deadpan humour filtered through the lyrics of *Dare* adding a subliminal sense of silliness which contemporaries like Gary Numan, Visage, Ultravox and Adam Ant were entirely devoid of; and the girls really *did* look like they'd just been plucked from a provincial disco floor.

Was the effect to de-mystify the proceedings of pop? Or was that the wishful thinking of critics? One of the earliest and best Fast 45s had been the Gang Of Four's EP *Damaged Goods*. It featured a section in which one of the participants intoned an inventory of the prices and processes involved in creating the record.

The League's self-mocking tinge was effectively a revision of these tactics, enabling them to prosper in the mass market, something which they emphatically wanted to do. No, they were hardly innocents. But at the same time they approached pop as theory with an upstart impudence which ended up approximating it. Everyone's enrolled in a media studies course these days, even if it's only to the extent of watching old movies on TV, and without doubt the best of the Human League's output since *Dare* has happened when this hick sense of mischief held sway. As with the likeable (and subsequently highly durable) Depeche Mode, their appeal was that of bright out-of-towners getting hold of new technology's toys and making them work. The Modes, with their genuinely tender years and fluttering silicon pop made more convincing babes in the (Basildon) woods than Phil and the team. The League, though, gave off a winning aroma of weaving throwaway finery around thoroughly unfashionable backgrounds. Sheffield, it must be said, is hardly San Tropez, and it's not exactly Brixton either.

Musically, 1984's *Louise* (taken from the *Hysteria* album) is the only post-*Dare* piece to contain its own satirical undertow within the actual song. It is the most lugubrious League love lament, a work of elaborately feigned sentiment concerning the possible reconciliation of former partners. *Louise* availed itself of the public eye by a combination of a bus, a working men's cafe, and an unconcealed Yorkshire accent. The monochrome video gave us Oakey aboard the house boat of Virgin Records' boss, surrounded by rows and rows and *rows* of books containing, we are teasingly urged, nothing but Philip's poetic tributes to she he longs to please. The bus does a racing skid stop on a canal bridge. The entire project is an exercise in downbeat absurdity which also works as a plastic flower of romance.

Mirror Man and *(Keep Feeling) Fascination* a pair of one-off singles between LPs were, on the other hand, just infectious Motown pastiches. Any jibing double meaning cropped up in the videos rather than the songs themselves, and it was Steve Barron's piece accompanying the latter which focused most clearly on the delighted confidence of a group who had 'made it' on an international scale.

From a red dot on a road map, the camera homes in on a street corner house in an urban slum. The house, and circular space around it, have been painted red, a joke translation of the map dot into real life. Nosing through the front room, we find the group in a tiny grey-blue room wielding grey-blue instruments. They are all dressed in black, and smeared in eye pencil and rouge. They 'perform' the song straight . . . almost. The camera homes in on a series of winks, laughs and secret smiles. A brilliant evocation of backstreet Glam, the video highlighted all the best impulses that had only been implied before. These people were interlopers, not city slickers. They weren't from clubland, but from discoland, an antidote to the capital's ghastly cavalcade of art pseuds; 'normals' enjoying the egalitarian fantasy of instant, easy fame.

But the one-dimensional perfection of *Mirror Man* and *Fascination* also pinpointed future failings of the Human League, problems which their next album *Hysteria* would reveal. So seamless was *Dare* that anything else in its wake was bound to appear flawed. Apart from anything else, the League fell foul of a new pop Catch 22 which had throttled others before them. The manufacture of a flawless formula leaves nowhere else to go. To copy simply provokes boredom, but to change is to break the spell.

Hysteria sounded bewildered in the face of this. Real bass and guitars appeared to break the synth monopoly, and there were some strong songs. But the album's creation was thwarted by bad luck which forced a change of producer half-way through (Rushent's only involvement was to assist with drum programming), and there was a certain lack of *mischief*. How ironic for a group who'd traded in irony to fine effect that, discounting *Louise*, the best track was the least flirtatious. *Life On Your Own* simply detailed isolation, and capped everything with a genuinely moving chorus. Released as a single, it inspired a clever Simon Milne video in which the viewer follows Oakey as he wanders through heaps of rubbish in an empty Wembley Stadium or picks clothes off the peg in an empty department store. By re-reading the lyric as apocalyptic rather than romantic, the League's endless interest in the mounting debris of urban western living was maintained. So too was its obsession with media cliché; and more striking than anything is the shot of the song's protagonist gazing wistfully at flickering TV sets, his nearest thing to contact with other human life.

What a wonderfully symbolic inverse to the clip for *Don't You Want Me?*, where small and large screen mannerisms had been cut up and re-arranged with delight. Now, viewing tacky TV re-runs was an accompaniment to depression. Within a couple of years the re-cyclable ghosts of pop's past had turned out to be a finite resource.

Alas for the bogus 'futurism'. So much for the synthesiser as the sound of tomorrow. The silicon chip continues to be touted as a glimpse of the future in your hands today, but just as so much science fiction indicates a craving for some mythic golden age, so the Human League's points of reference were exclusively the flotsam of history. In the absence of progress, all that remained was the prospect of eternally juggling with symbols and signs: Gary Glitter, T.Rex, Flash Gordon, Diamond Dogs, Daleks, The Man From Uncle, lovingly preserved bubblegum cards . . . you name it, it made a fey appearance somewhere along the line. The Human League's progress finally revealed how introverted pop could easily become; and how paralysed. In view of this, the League's most recent departure into solidly commercial dance-floor material with the capable Flyte Tyme production team makes solid sense. With tunesmith Callis and original patron Bob Last gone, 'quality pop' may be the best they can now attain; artful fakerists no more.

At their peak, the group's critics derided them for feigning innocence, but that's only half the truth. At their best, they examined the bankruptcy of pop's ways and means, relished its triviality and let us watch them doing it. That's been the grown-up's thrill with '80s pop, also its indictment. The Human League gave us both sides of the coin. At the end of the day their lesson is summed up by Philip Oakey's response to an assertion that they were a very different concoction to Bucks Fizz. 'Are we?' Philip said. It's really quite a thought.

14

▓▓

FRANKIE GOES TO HOLLYWOOD
The Last Great Apocalyptic Pop Swindle

'The world is my oyster,' proclaimed Holly Johnson in the elaborate prelude to *Welcome To The Pleasuredome*, and up until that moment he'd been right.

Everything, every tiny little detail, about Frankie Goes To Hollywood's brief and blistering rise had been absolutely right. It had been more right than just about anything before, the ultimate allegory of pop. For a start, they were greedy. Extremely greedy. Just think about the name. There's nothing shy about that. They wanted to be fêted and admired, and very rich indeed. 'It's really obvious isn't it, what's attractive about success,' Paul Rutherford said: 'it's like a little dream that always seems unreachable, and when you find yourself on the first rungs of the ladder, it's like, very, very nice. It doesn't *mean* anything really. It's just our little need. We don't want to be evil about it. We just wanna do it.'

The original legend of the name is that it came from a photo in an old magazine of Frank Sinatra 'de-planing' at Los Angeles, and being mobbed by gaggles of teeny boppers. A mythology has been abstracted from it since: 'adapted for television,' in Holly Johnson's words, 'Frankie Goes To Hollywood' became a metaphor for one plain lad's voyage of discovery. Hollywood would become more than Frankie's televisual escape. It would become his *total* escape, in fact his salvation, his *new* reality. And he'd do *anything* to get there.

It had come as a revelation to learn that Brian Epstein bought the first Beatles single into the bottom end of the chart. But that's all different now. Corruption is blithely accepted chicanery, legit. To be honest is to be a square and a bore, but villainy is style. Malcolm McLaren had blagged the Pistols into folklore, hit records, large sums of cash, *and he bragged about it*. It's not the *doing* so much as the gloating and the Coming Out. McLaren is eulogised, fawned over, while Sid Vicious lies in the ground. The confidence trickster is the modern hero. So when staid people said that Frankie Goes To Hollywood are all very fine, but they can't play their instruments, can they? they weren't seeing through the scam, they were pissing in the wind, because the scam was the core of Frankie's *raison d'être*. The mechanics of manipulation are now part of the entertainment – fiddling dressed up as Art.

Frankie Goes To Hollywood were happy to be fiddled with if there was something in it for them. At the start, their function was to throw the postures and come up with the raw ideas for songs. Everything else was to be shared between Trevor and Paul. What a pair they were. Mr Horn did the epic production jobs, and

Rutherford, child and T-shirt in the image of '84.

Mr Morley wound up the press. The boys in the band were the faces, the frontispiece. For the creation of a bit of folk devilry, they had all the right component parts. The gender-bender roller coaster was galloping towards the point when someone came right out and said the unsayable. So Rutherford and Johnson did. They weren't the drag queens or mincing panto 'poofters' the great British public were used to. They were a new kind of homosexual cartoon: sweating gay cropheads in leather vests, out to scare you half to death. The other three fulfilled another unsettling story brought to life – the Lads, a trio of mad, bad scallys on the rampage.

So between them, Horn, Morley, and the Scouse quintet came up with the last great pop idea. And although Wham! overtook them in the final weeks – and what an indication of things to come – 1984 belonged to Frankie Goes To Hollywood. They virtually took over the country, subjecting us to the most pervasive marketing campaign in pop history. And with *Two Tribes* they gave us the grand slam: sex, horror, glamour, hype, outrage, quality and cash. . .and built-in obsolescence.

Up until *Pleasuredome* finally hit the record racks, the Frankie saga had been the most immaculately executed piece of theory into practice ever. Only a devoted student of pop as plot and pleasure could have dreamed the whole thing up. Hence, Paul Morley, critic turned propagandist. 'We wanted to create a teenybop dream. It's the last teenybop dream in a way, and one that belongs in an '80s context. All those teenybop successes like Kershaw and Heyward and all those idiots are so wet they could belong to the '60s. But in the '70s I always thought the teenybop bands of the '80s would be horrific, cos kids in the '80s would have so much stimuli, so much lust. That's what we've noticed in all the letters written to Frankie Goes To Hollywood from fourteen-year-old-girls; they all want to fuck the band, every single one. They want little bags of sperm.'

It was Morley who chose the name for Frankie's record label. ZTT stands for Zang Tuum Tumb. The name is stolen from a work by the Italian futurist Filippo Tommaso Marinetti, an acknowledged expert at packaging, who believed, in the early twentieth century, that machinery would set humanity free. (He later became a fascist, which you can take as you will.) Everything from artwork to press communiqués to the style of the artists' clothes was subjected to Morley's rapacious attention.

And who can deny he knew what he was up to? Morley had both the know-how and the will to create a spectacle. As a writer with the then declining pacemaker of the weekly rock papers, the *New Musical Express*, he had exhibited both an insight into the ways and means of post-punk music and a capacity for self-promotion which were hard to ignore. He, more than anyone, gave Frankie's hit reign the aspect of a crusade.

But ZTT is Trevor Horn's operation in the end. It's not so much a record company as a production outlet for the most ostentatiously successful studio svengali of recent years. In 1979, partnered by Geoff Downes, Horn had given Island Records their first number one single with *Video Killed The Radio Star*, working under the assumed name of the Buggles. The record's sentiment and antiseptic finish today look like an omen. By 1983 Horn had scored notable successes with clever ABC, and with Dollar, a male-female duo possessing the mail order aura of the newly engaged. He'd revamped ailing mid-'70s 'progressive' band Yes, and liaised with none other than Malcolm McLaren on a musicological novelty album called *Duck Rock*.

In search of a studio to call his own, Horn's bygone contact with Island gave him the chance to take over their one-time house studio in Basing Street, Notting Hill. ZTT was created as an imprint for his work there. Island would handle promotion and distribution of what, it seemed fair to anticipate, would be a very lucrative operation indeed.

Frankie Goes To Hollywood were precisely the type of group to bring the best out of Horn. Technically primitive, they nonetheless had a few decent songs, which combined the hard riffs of rock with the homophonic thump of hi-energy disco, the subterranean soundtrack of the established gay club scene – total studio music. Production was close to everything with this type of sound, and Horn's is the kind of input which plays as obtrusive a part in the final product as that of the artists he works with. In the tradition of Phil Spector and Giorgio Morodor he applies a customised coating of sound which defines the final quality. Crystal clear, richly textured, mock symphonic – the optimum qualities for the hi-tech sound system of discotheque and home.

Completing the ZTT triumvirate there was his wife and business partner Jill Sinclair whose reputation as a driver of hard bargains is second to none. So keen were the Frankie boys to get in on the act that they too entered into the grand heritage of pop – the group's three composers signed a publishing contract for a less than spectacular £5,000 and as a unit obtained an advance of £250 for each of their first two singles. They went into the studio with the bespectacled perfectionist and prayed for a hit.

Against this hidden background then, unfolds the remarkable tale of Frankie Goes To Hollywood, a story of two startling singles and an orgy of media situationism without precedent. The whole idea was simply to renovate every thread in the tapestry of pop. Every marketing ploy ever employed would be taken to new and extravagant extremes. Every tired double standard of the entertainment establishment would be exposed yet again, as if by ritual. The age-old story of social lepers outraging moral values only to transform into institutional scenery would be repeated and completed inside a year. In short, Frankie would be the supreme in-joke and the matchless exemplification of pop hyperbole making good once again.

The thing was not to stand by and jeer, but to join in the game, obliterate the old boys and leave with the spoils. For Morley, Frankie would be his revenge on all the stars to shine after Punk had died away. 'All those groups like Spandau Ballet and Duran Duran were just going into record company marketing departments and doing what they were told,' he stormed. 'They might use pretty little designs of their own, but they weren't doing anything fundamentally to knock it all sideways. All it required was an intelligent new way of selling records. Our philosophy was to go in there and compete, and show that it can be done better.'

And do it better they certainly did. After a few weeks of stumbling around in the middle of the top 100, *Relax*, the first Frankie Goes To Hollywood single (and the first ZTT release), finally got to number 35. Once the vital top forty barrier had been breached, every cliché of pop sensationalism seemed to step forward and take an encore.

First of all, Bernard Rose's video was deemed unsuitable for broadcast by the BBC. Set in a leather bar, the promo transposes Frankie's philosophy into moving pictures. Johnson, the innocent, is lured into a world of sin by Rutherford. The Lads all make fleeting appearances. Morley delivers Johnson to the bar's entrance in a rickshaw, sporting a pair of Mickey Mouse ears. Bondage images abound. All in all, far less offensive than half the rape fantasy titillations which are the bread and butter of many video directors, but there you were – it would never do to have this kind of song (thong?) on *Top Of The Pops*.

Suitable censored, the band faked their way through the first *TOTP* of the new year. Already usefully touched by controversy, they leapt to number six the following week, whereupon Radio One DJs began paying serious attention for the first time. Breakfast show host Mike Read, unveiling the latest chart, made his famous pronouncement that he would not play the biggest climber on the chart that week because he considered it 'overtly obscene', and seven days later, *Relax* was at number one.

As Read's outburst prompted both BBC radio and television to impose a blanket ban on the most popular record in the United Kingdom, the party really began to swing.

What, exactly, did we have on our hands? In the first place, something quite ridiculous. How *could* the state broadcasting networks possibly make such fools of themselves *again*? The song had received a quota of airplay *before* it cracked the chart which was, if anything, generous for an unknown act's first effort. Now the public were voting with their wallets it was decided that they'd better not be allowed to hear it any more.

This was not the same thing as the censorship of the Sex Pistols who were already notorious before they released *God Save The Queen*. *Relax*'s exposure amounted to sessions for David Jensen and John Peel, some evening radio spins, a fair amount of press coverage, and a couple of appearances on *The Tube*. Now, backed into a corner by the ludicrous rantings of Read, Frankie became an Event, a Cause. They stayed at the top for five consecutive weeks.

Relax was certainly a powerful record. Its ingredients were faithfully represented in an end result which mixed crudity with sophistication and a sweltering splash of ravenous sex. It was a *hungry* sound, and the pop scene had really missed it. But making good records is only the spade work in the cultivation of a true pop palaver. It is the paraphernalia, the fallout from giant sales which confirms an act as a *phenomenon*. ZTT paid as much attention to the flotsam as they had the actual product. Every inch a theoretician, Morley's entirely upfront manipulation of Fleet Street's gutless gullibility proved what a (pseudo) intellectual activity the pop process had become. But Morley could also boast a moral conviction. 'My personal philosophy is to communicate with as many people as possible,' he explained at the height of Frankie's Summer of Lust; 'because I think they are abused something rotten. I think their vocabulary is diluted, and that the amount of choice they have about what they take into their lives is enormously inhibited. Pop music seems to be a great way to bust that apart.'

The currency of Frankie's communiqué was sensationalism, and *Relax* offered a fresh variation on sex as a shock value staple. After years of transvestitism and camp we finally got unapologetic, homosexuality fetishised. After years of phallic posturing, heavy breathing and hang-on-in-and-get-on-down innuendo, somebody got to the point — Frankie said 'come'.

It was text book stuff. Once the powers that be had taken the bait it was just a question of sticking by the rules. Morley gave everyone whatever they wanted. 'You cannot communicate without sensationalism because the entire nation's media relies on sensationalism. We hate videos and all that rubbish, but unfortunately we're stuck with it now. So our philosophy is to go in there and compete, to do it better, to do it *richer*.'

Frankie Goes To Hollywood were a declaration that Punk's independent ethos had run out of credence. Although the Pistols had been the classic hype with a destructive streak, Punk had also inspired the rebirth of the small record label as an antidote to the rich and wasteful majors and their rich and wasteful bands. Like the Pistols, the Frankies didn't play too well either. But the flaunting of poverty, either technical or financial, was not in their brochure. Instead, ZTT gave them a gilded veneer, lavishing them in every promotional, marketing and packaging indulgence. Gleefully, ZTT pursued everything to extremes of absurdity. Frankie became a metaphor for guiltless opulence, their journey a craven chase after luxury and plenty. So when Frankie Goes To Hollywood made 12-inch versions of their singles in limited editions to help boost sales, you didn't just get the 7-inch version with bits stuck on the front and back, you bought the complete re-mix with the whole new features edited in. What's more, the 12-inch wasn't just a one-off. With the second single *Two Tribes*, extended alternative takes saturated the market in a quite naked (and entirely Gallup-proof) attempt to keep the song at the top of the chart.

How people *squealed* about what was, after all, nothing but an extension of already established principles. Even apparently sane music critics complained that Horn's *Two Tribes* production was 'over the top'. *Of course* it was over the top! The entire

The Freddie Mercury fan club pre-Hollywood 1983.

Frankie ideology revolved around the desire to push standard practices into the realm of the ridiculous. You want videos? Here's a Godley and Creme creation costing £60,000 featuring a prize fight skit on the Cold War featuring Reagan and Chernenko lookalikes and a snickering Holly broadcasting its progress to the world. Sleeve information? Here's a bunch of unattributed quotes about alcoholism in Russia, homosexuality in the American armed forces, and dubious figures about who's got what missiles aimed at who. As Frankie parodied consumption, they also celebrated it. Indeed, they revelled in all the joys of enjoyment. 'Though both Boy George and Bowie are gorgeous boys – if you like that sort of thing,' Holly told *Him Monthly* in January '84, 'they're working in a grey area, they're playing with androgyny. But we're black and white. There's no pussy-footing with us. We are into PLEASURE and we think that what has been regarded as a sexual perversion should be brought into the open.'

The first two FGTH records gathered up all the great preoccupations of their time, and sold them back as excitement and satire. *Relax* luxuriated in its robotic sensuality, the pumping body language of the male only gymnasium; sheer homoerotic hedonism. *Two Tribes* mocked the rhetoric of Ronald Reagan (impressionist Chris Barrie made the surreal speeches) and employed Patrick Allen (the hectoring voice of Barratt Homes and *Protect And Survive*) to send up Britain's guidelines for post-holocaust living: 'mine is the last voice that you will ever hear. Do not be alarmed.' Sex, horror, sex, horror, sex. Yes, these were the new Gods, just like the record said.

'When you look back at ZTT from 1993,' opined Morley; 'you'll know what the '80s were all about. You know, all these questions and justifications and how everyone's so fucking confused.' It could be claimed that *Relax* and *Two Tribes* were protest songs. But in their soul Frankie were past protesting. Protest was for people who worried about things. Even the *Wall Street Journal*, who you'd think might know leisure capitalism when they saw it, described Frankie as a 'leftist rock band'. They were, of course, neither 'rock' nor 'leftist'. Frankie's 'politics', their resolution to the messy paranoias of the world, was the pursuit of dangerous enjoyment, the total submission to desire. The enemy was anyone who threatened that pursuit. *Two Tribes* proposed ridicule, not the taking of sides. 'It's not political,' insisted Holly, 'it sounds *glorious* I think.'

In *Two Tribes* the idea of the apocalypse became a festival of black comic erotica – ooh, the Big Bang! – showing us once more what a hot commodity Armageddon has become. Johnson didn't worry about that, the scandal surrounding him, anything. 'I don't really care about things like that. I think it was a good song. I am satisfied with the quality of the product we have put out, and that's the only sort of credibility I need. I think the record company have made more effort than us, but that's alright isn't it? There are no rules are there? So any way you can sell an idea is a morally sound way.'

Morley expressed the belief that Frankie transcended moral and political arguments. But really, they simply avoided them. It was pointless to think about such things: 'It's hard to say what's right and wrong,' Paul Rutherford told *Record Mirror*'s Betty Page; 'obviously you have to draw the line at certain things. . .but it's hard to say who's moral and who's immoral.'

Frankie's was the sound of taking the cash. By October 1984 they had scored number one hits in fourteen different countries, including most of Europe, New Zealand, Thailand and Israel. One week before its release on October 29th an astounding 1.1 million copies of *Welcome To The Pleasuredome* had been ordered up by British retailers. It was impossible to move for *Relax* T-shirts (said to be the only direct source of income for the group before 1986) or variations on the 'Frankie

Says' theme – 'War! Hide Yourself!' 'Arm the Unemployed' ('arm the unemployed with *jobs*,' smirked Holly on Breakfast TV) – all of them dreamed up by Morley, pirating a design first created by Katherine Hamnett. The tabloids clamoured for their daily fix. Morley was delighted to oblige. *Two Tribes* stayed at number one for a ridiculous *nine* weeks on end.

Commerce, deviance, mischief, celebrity – Frankie Goes To Hollywood parcelled it all up. 'What we tried to do in terms of building the dream was get a band that goes to number one, but still be a band that people think is *theirs*,' expounded Morley; 'people see things in Frankie that seem like a secret to them. They're a pop band, they're a cult band, they're a club band, they're a gay band, and they're incredibly popular and *that's* the point. It slowly builds up and becomes invincible.'

He was right, and the industry adored him for it. 'With Frankie,' said Phil Cooper, Managing Director of Island International; 'we had a *dream* of a campaign. It was an incredible thing.' Douglas Coates, then Marketing Manager for the HMV record shop chain, said he considered Morley to be a whizz kid, a leading light in the renovation of the business at large after the disasters of the late '70s. 'In the future I think companies will market groups along the lines of Frankie;' he said. 'They'll be planned for periods of enormous success but over a very short time.'

The greatest returns in the history of pop have come when a maverick talent is neutralised just enough for it to be sold to the masses. ZTT demolished the time lapse between buying and selling. With Frankie, the apparently contradictory blend of renegade impulse and shopfront presentation came ready-mixed and tailor-made. They were *proud* to be consumer rebels.

Can pop culture contain its own critique? Frankie's little coups and ripples were giggly and illuminating. What a delight to feel the BBC's embarrassment as *Two Tribes* breezed to number one inside a week; as daft old Peter Powell (who, with producer Dave Atkey was the first to actually withdraw *Relax* from his programme on grounds of taste) fawned over every note ('He's trying to be nice, a bit liberal,' said Rutherford; 'but it's a bit sickening really'); as the voice of the fake Ronald Reagan boomed from the radio minutes after a news bulletin announcing his arrival on British soil; as *Relax* suddenly went back up the singles chart, all the way to number two.

But what *else* was there? 'To me, people are just stimulated by the first exhibition of genuine exuberance for a long time. It was energy,' said Morley; 'it was beyond definition. But now we've got it, we're gonna strangle it. Usually a number one group just gets there and tries to protect it. *We* have a kamikaze attitude to it. That's something that's got lost a little bit in pop. Everyone's just prepared to protect their success because they're scared of losing it. It's a neurotic thing, and a very selfish thing.'

But for all the stunts and manoeuvres and exposures, the finish of the Frankie adventure remains routine. By Christmas '84 the leathers and the studs were a long way in the past replaced by smart casuals, walking canes, tartan trousers, wardrobes from South Molton Street. Suavely, they swanned into film premières. Coolly, Rutherford posed for the cover of *The Face*. Blithely, Holly told BBC 1's Saturday peak time viewers that 'Terry Wogan's got green eyes.' None of these things were out of sympathy with the conspiracy itself. They just showed where it inevitably all ended up. Holly's tease of Terry was the last glimmer of cheek, the last bit of behind-the-hand signifying to be seen.

Welcome To The Pleasuredome was a double album for the price of one, but not worth the price of a single. Filching its title from Samuel Coleridge's *Kubla Khan*, it postured as a trip into a glorious underworld of sin and excess. Yet side one was just the singles re-hashed. Another was simply sub-standard original material. The side comprising cover versions, including their renditions of Bruce Springsteen's tearaway *Born To Run* and the Liverpool anthem *Ferry Cross The Mersey* was unexceptional even as a camp joke. The title track, meanwhile, was attractive enough, but hardly the thrill of the century. And with it, for the first time, Frankie really *did* look like Trevor's puppets at last.

Previously, the satire at the heart of the Frankie operation had made that accusation redundant (not to say unfair. They might not have been the RPO, but Brian Nash, Mark O'Toole and Peter 'Ped' Gill *could* hold down a tune – just). The key was the bare-faced nature of the leg-pulling, the way they made all the DJs (but Peel, who actually discovered them, and Jensen) look daft, the way they got away with it without bothering to cover up. And ultimately everything was justified by the quality. *Relax* was a very good record. *Two Tribes* is one of the most stunning of recent times. Everything about it and everything around it says everything about pop in this decade.

But a group defined by product power has nothing left when that power fails. *The Power Of Love* was a dreary follow up, and *Pleasuredome* pales miserably by comparison to those first two epic adventures on 45. Frankie went to Hollywood, but they didn't go very far. The best thing about their US tour was the time and place it started: Washington on Presidential election day. It was their last piece of perfect timing, the last time we saw any hint of Morley's promised kamikaze ploys.

They stopped winning too, which was just as fatal to a unit like this one. The bloated concept album refused to leave the shops after it had comprehensively invaded them, and was ultimately eclipsed by that of soon-to-be British cultural emissaries, George and Andrew of well-mannered Wham! Even the prospect of mail-ordering FGTH Jean Genet boxer shorts couldn't compensate for *Make It Big*'s appeal, and when the Frankie boys turned up to do *Relax* on Christmas *Top Of The Pops*, you wondered what all the fuss had been about. Belatedly the Beeb won out by turning the other cheek.

Frankie Goes To Hollywood and ZTT illustrate by example the limitations of pop as an Idea. You may invent a different route, but your destination is the same. The only way to subvert from within is to turn round and go back again. But Frankie liked Hollywood a little bit too much in the end. They showed us that the only thing smarter than average interventionists can do that all the others can't is become redundant icons at a faster rate.

Frankie played pop-as-conspiracy theory better than anyone, but ended up overkilled and dreary just the same. So Holly will get into movies, the Lads will be accidental millionaires, and Paul Rutherford will carry on shrugging. *Two Tribes* started with an Air Attack warning siren: 'A lot of kids thought that was the flood warning,' said the latter, offhand. Did people get the point? How many of those fourteen-year-old-girls got past writing in for 'little bags of sperm?'

There was one man who found a use for *Welcome To The Pleasuredome* – nightclub owner Peter Stringfellow, another northern working boy made good. He discovered it was perfect to accompany his newest venture's special, spectacle light show. Watching it, you realised that the world was not Holly's oyster at all. It was his Hippodrome. Unless you're flush or famous or freaky enough to be admitted as scenery, you can't get in. Frankie did – but he will never get out again.

15

||||||||||||||||||||||||||||||||||||||||||||||||||||||||||||||||||||||||||||||||||||||||||||||||||||||||||||||||||||||||||||

CULTURE CLUB
Enter the Agony Aunt

Like a panto Terry Wogan or a peacetime Vera Lynn, the Boy appeared from nowhere just when his country needed him. How thrilling he was to behold, this universal sugared pill, this enema for the inertia of public angst, this incorrigible provider of comfort and of joy. One way or another, who could possibly resist?

The Sting had grown up and left the fold. Adam Ant, showbiz pop perfectionist, had been the first post-punk dandy to espouse the virtues of conventional entertainment values, but his star was swift to fade, its light not bright enough to reach far beyond the Top Forty world. The Boy, though, burst upon the scene like a cryptic Pierrot from the underworld, a one-man camp cavalcade. We were already used to the newly overt narcissism of pop, and its set of standards promoting highly privatised realms of enjoyment. But though people had heard of Steve Strange and seen his fancy clothes, it was hard to snuggle up to a businessman in drag. They needed something more. And with Boy George and Culture Club, pop's new tree of life truly began to bloom.

The Boy took the burgeoning cult of visibility and turned it into a national resource. It came so *naturally* to him. For years, from chaotic Catholic childhood to his now thoroughly documented days as a garish nightclub crasher, George had practised the fine art of cultivating attention. Swimming with disarming ostentation against whatever tide prevailed, he had refined his technique within a tawdry London sub-culture of disenfranchised pleasure-seekers, would-be commercial artists and a new generation of youthful gays. As the party began to spread into the mainstream, George revealed himself as a goldmine of bright ideas, was garrulous with it, and, once set up with a band and the backing of Virgin Records, skilfully arranged a mass-market manifesto for himself.

George seemed to know precisely what to do. The first Culture Club hit, *Do You Really Want To Hurt Me?* captured everything to perfection. You could almost hear the singer's eyebrows flutter as he cooed a lyric which anticipated hostility to his outlandish, androgynous appearance, and simultaneously sought to defuse it in a knowing display of utter harmlessness. George nurtured the public gawp through a winning combination of weirdness and friendliness. Instantly he transformed himself into an object for debate. Down market newspapers desperate to cram their pages with extraordinary 'personalities' to counter-balance the ongoing misery which dominated their headlines, threw themselves in the Boy's direction, the most marvellous creature to crawl out of the woodwork yet. How delighted George must

The Boy in self-contemplation. Tussauds scene captured by Kerstin Rodgers.

have been: after his first appearance on *Top Of The Pops*, the *Sun* dubbed him Wally Of The Week, but Britain's youngest hailed him as a hero. Divided in its reactions, the nation was united in its fascination, and a superstar was born.

Pop continues to be dismissed as trivial and trite. But as a commodity Culture Club were sophisticated and intelligent. George's quest was for absolute accessibility, and its achievement demanded multiple points of reference. The way the group portrayed them is explained by its name; they presented themselves as a brochure for the underprivileged universe, a society where every kind of outcast could theoretically find a place of entry. And at the core of the mélange sat the winking, beckoning figure of the Boy George himself.

In its search for frills and embellishments, the singer's magpie eye left nothing sacred. The look comprised a jumble of symbols and images including gypsy scarves, stars of David, bucketfuls of make-up, as well as Rastafarian colours, hat and artificial locks. It typified the craze for displaced cultural eclecticism which so dominated contemporary pop. The band's three other members reinforced the cosmopolitan theme. Drummer Jon Moss was dark and jewish; guitarist Roy Hay, fair and anglo-saxon; bassist Mikey Craig, black. Delicately, effectively their early sound melted together in a kaleideoscope of musics: funk and reggae rhythms, latin percussion, soul-inflected vocals and the melodic constructions of pop. A collage of many colours and shapes, this utterly untroubled cross-fertilisation exuded a simple, pristine prettiness. Its naivety did not undermine it, but compounded its appeal. Hearing the early Culture Club was effortless, like breathing a sigh of relief. It was a noise filled with promise – and the singer looked like a girl.

The debut album *Kissing To Be Clever* (1982) showcased these 'dreadlock demons of the dance' and confirmed the firm impression that the Boy liked nothing more than to stir up speculation. There was no attempt to deflect prying eyes; George positively encouraged them. Every song had him either singing to himself, or moralising on the folly of judging a person by their appearance. He teased us and he told us off; at once he demanded to be set apart and accepted as the same. Here was the paradoxical essence of George's booming saleability, and his chart-topping successes reflected as much as anything a rank-and-file request for the new face to explain himself. The Boy needed no second bidding. Never short of words, in his total celebrity repertoire, there was a crisply gabbed gift for anyone who asked. As the video for *Hurt Me* implied, with its opening cabaret courtroom scene, George welcomed audience judgement; and their verdict was that enquiries should go on and on and on.

There had been a couple of failed singles before that lilting, flirtatious number one, but now he had claimed the limelight, George moved to prove to the masses that he was opinionated and articulate, a true media marvel who could re-invent himself in a near-infinity of different combinations. Though a non-conformist, George broke with poprock tradition by being devoid of a threatening physical presence. An alluring, glamorous and amorous being, he managed to project virtually no sexual identity at all so complete was his transcendence of gender expectations. Indeed, George made sex seem incredibly simple; everything about him implied that he simply *wasn't that interested*. 'I don't think they fancy me in a sexual sort of way.' he opined of his fans to an excited *Daily Mirror*; 'I wouldn't like *that*.' How *thrilled* everyone was when they heard!

George endeared himself to all kinds of folk. To the *Coronation Street* faithful (among whom he counted himself) he could be lined up alongside giant-sized camp atrocities like Liberace and Barry Manilow as the middle-aged housewive's choice. As a cuddly toy boy pin-up friend he flew with comparable directness to the core of pre-teen schoolgirl hearts. At the height of his fame, a series of shows at the

Dominion, London, were packed with lovingly turned-out under-thirteens in lovingly pressed print frocks, hats and braids. They squealed, they cheered, they even swooned as George pouted and pirouetted through his party paces. But no pubescent undies were directed at the stage, because with George such traumatic complications simply failed to arise.

Before very long, the band were honing their jamboree bag approach into flawless pastiche. What was original about George was not his vision of the world but his aptitude for picking its pockets. The result was, and remains, that Culture Club deal in impressions rather than specifics. As befitted a man in search of grand-scale attention rather than the meaning of life, George was a pirate of surface appearances, and he was all his own work. While bearing every known hallmark of a novelty act, no-one manufactured him, his Look or his songs except himself. His was a maverick impulse with a marketing department built-in.

The high Culture Club gloss was most brilliantly applied to the contents of their second LP, 1983's *Colour By Numbers*. Bolstered by the higher profile of the tough-voiced Helen Terry, the album offers smart renovations of the gospel dynamic, and the slick, clipped beat of Tamla Motown in its prime, all doused in the Club's dream topping sound. From Steve Levine's clean, uncluttered production to Assorted iMaGes' primary colour scheme on the sleeve, *Colour By Numbers* appeals like a box of soft-centred sweets.

The whole package just exudes supreme professional confidence. It's this that gives it a conviction you would imagine to be at odds with so light and flyaway a thing. But then that's classic Culture Club, and archetypal George. As with all good advertisements, throwaway fragments insinuate a desirable mood, and the mood of *Colour* is splashy and friendly and vibrant and ultimately one of absolute triumph. Culture Club had swiftly followed the Human League, Soft Cell and Junior into the American charts, and all their trappings now reflected this international dimension to a fabulous underdog victory. The album's cover shows each of the three musicians hooped by an approximation of an olympic ring, contributing to the cover art's subliminal sporting theme. Linked symbols for male and female make a repeat appearance, but this time forming the borders to distant views of the Planet Earth. The video for the first single off the album, *Church Of The Poison Mind* (the very *sheerest* Tamla) is just as firmly stamped with the seal of success. The boys and girl appear hanging out of a chrome-encrusted open-topped American saloon, and play-acting in a mock-up of an aeroplane cockpit. The overwhelming sense of the English jet-setting it abroad is formalised by a James Bond 'eye' – not the last time the 007 heritage would be invoked in the videos of the new, internationalist UK pop.

Logical objections stood little chance against this surge of exuberance. It was such an *attractive* ascent. The easy feeling of *Colour By Numbers* exemplified the core of Culture Club's appeal at the time. Music of effortless, deceptive simplicity was borne from a cacophony of apparent irreconcilables; men and women, black and white, poor and rich. Contradictions were simply shown the door. Even George, who by any standard yardstick of 'normality' should have been some dangerous kind of deviant, was very plainly Mr Affable himself. 'Black and white pop for child's ears', ran an early advertising slogan, and Culture Club were the nearest thing to a genuine sense of innocence we would get at the height of the second British pop boom. This was life as primary colours, and how pleasurable it was to give in to. Right from the start George had grasped the fundamentals of his own attraction; and *Colour By Numbers* proved it. Pop is rarely more skilfully or seductively wrought than this. An indispensible LP.

Part of Boy George's secret has been to allow specialised input from others into his career, so long as it doesn't detract from the glorification of himself. Is it purely coincidence that once a third party is accorded credit for some aspect of his success, they tend to be dispensed with? What became of *Kissing To Be Clever* designer Sue Clowes? Why did Helen Terry last so short a time in the limelight? Malcolm Garrett and Kaspar DeGraaf of Assorted iMaGes have always remained modest about their involvement. Is that why they've survived so long? They aren't going to be drawn. Boy George, it appears, doesn't care for too much competition from within, so it was poetically apt that as his celebrity soared he began to take on a status which separated him from the rest of the group. The cosy video for *Time*, Culture Club's second UK hit, had closed with the band watching themselves on TV while a mother figure brought them hot drinks in individual mugs, each bearing the appropriate band member's name. George was the star all right, but clearly one of a tight quartet. Now, with the legend of George O'Dowd existing as an independent entity, the Boy's public persona became more and more that of a narrator, a commentator, a figure on the outside looking in. With his knack for attracting attention outlasting the paparazzi's short-term shock logic, he got the chance to

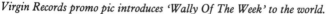

Virgin Records promo pic introduces 'Wally Of The Week' to the world.

pronounce not merely on himself but on the world at large.

Whether by coincidence or contrivance, Culture Club videos began to confirm George's onlooker's gaze, and at the same time started to reflect the group's standing as entertainers who reached beyond the traditional pop market of youth. *Karma Chameleon*, another number one hit, was melodically emphatically middle-of-the-road. In the accompanying promo a straight narrative, set on an 1870s Mississippi steamboat, replaced the more usual frenzy of cross-cut images; and while Craig, Moss and Hay all participate in the action, George looks on and spins the yarn. Similarly, Godley and Creme's grand camp sub-Berkleyesque creation for the lush, melodramatic and very lovely ballad *Victims* placed O'Dowd even further apart from the action of the song. The others play decidedly low-key parts in a production featuring a full orchestra and a black choir, which grandly celebrated George's elevation to total acclaim. Prim, spangled, topped with a huge hat, and playing everything to the hilt, the star serenades us with conspiratorial intimacy from the foreground.

Karma Chameleon was explained by George as an expression of his belief that as ye sow so shall ye reap. And, indeed, behind the extreme tastes and mannerisms that made his name lies a desire to portray and promote equilibrium. OK, he wore the odd wedding gown, and used the ladies powder room; but George still insisted on his basic conservatism.

'The most abnormal thing in the world is to want to look like everyone else,' he told a scintillated *Daily Express* in June '83; 'I feel sorry for those who laugh at me. I am only being an individual,' To a public speculating madly about his likely sexual habits, George blithely recommended platonic love over physical lust, declaring that a female friend he'd met in Japan (called Mika) and he had never made love. 'Oooh!' went the crowd. 'I think basically I'm a very moral person, and I have very traditional ideas about sexuality and love,' he pronounced, seemingly unblemished by doubt. George was wonderful that way.

With Boy George such sentimental, homespun truisms came ten-a-penny, and millions of eager voyeurs were ever ready for more. Coming as he did out of a backdrop of gender bender controversy, George all the more strikingly embodies for people what seemed unavailable in every other sphere of contemporary life – a sense of harmony and order. By the close of '83 he was already a household name, a figure as readily recognisable as Princess Di with whom he vied for front-page coverage. Arriving for tea at Claridges without a suit and tie, George was not ejected like anyone else would have been, but found a private room. His power as an institution was now sufficient for him to join Elvis Presley and the Beatles in Madame Tussaud's waxwork hall of fame. As the undisputed Alternative Queen Of England, George became a key ingredient in the great national distraction, feeding a rabid public ardour for soap, gossip, spectacle and more of all three. With every career move, every pose and quote, every holiday and tiff with his contemporary Marilyn, and with every whispy song, George did his bit for Britannia in her oh-so-troubled times.

George achieved rather more than simply maintaining Fame's greatest myth – that anyone can make it if they've got the willpower and the nerve. He expanded it to exemplify the idea of joy in the face of despair, personifying a seductive pretence of togetherness based entirely on *surfaces*. 'If I was in power I'd lean more towards ecology,' he said when quizzed about his political opinions; 'improving the environment people live in.' For Boy George *presentation* is the key to the quality of life, whatever tuneful aphorisms he has conjured to the contrary. He is the most perfectly polished example of how post-Punk pop reconciled itself to what rock'n'roll rhetoric compulsively excluded – that the process of selling is as much a part of the culture as what's being sold. Previously, the product tended to emerge as a compromise between corporate requirements and the capabilities or co-operativeness of the artists. Pop in the '80s has resolved this conflict with cool pragmatic charm. The most striking and inventive of the new stars have been as much the creators of their market profiles as the words they sing and the noises they make. Culture Club required precisely no remoulding to make them into a consumer item serving a multitude of needs. All they needed was the resources to make the blueprint work. Given a free hand, everything looked after itself, and George's glorious gift of natural stardom kicked the whole thing into overdrive.

As the latest brimming bearer of the Union Jack abroad, George soon brought America to heel. The latest example of Britain's winning way with a spectacle, he could scarcely fail as a walking, talking tourist attraction. Against all predictions he did the Stateside media double: thriving on an encounter with the right-wing queen bitch of TV chat Joan Rivers, and popping up on the front of *People* magazine. 'Pop Genius Or Freak, The Kids Are Getting His Message', ran the latter's cover line, though what the 'message' was, *People* made little attempt to reveal.

By the time Culture Club had conquered Europe and Japan as well as Britain and America, George had become little more than a metaphor for mad dog English eccentricity at large. Like Noel Coward he found himself in danger of delivering nothing to his watchers and admirers beyond the mere fact of his existence. The video accompanying the enchanting single *It's A Miracle* (the fourth 45 lifted from *Colour By Numbers*) celebrated the history of the group through the device of a giant dayglow board game. The interpretation was certainly apt. But where did they go now the game was won?

For the first time, Culture Club were found wanting. All of a sudden, everything that had been valuable, positive or just plain pleasurable for its cheek and style began to become swamped beneath the sheer weight of George's preposterous status. Achieving the camp coup of making the covers of both *Woman* and *Woman's Own* magazines, he became a purveyor of homilies, a kind of agony aunt of the non-specific issue. On anger: 'too many people bottle it up. Me, I'll throw something like a vase and smash it to pieces just to get it out of my system.' On outrage: 'most of the people *I* think are outrageous look really ordinary. I think character is very important – you can't wear a character.' And, famously, on sex: 'I'd rather have a cup of tea and a good conversation.' It didn't matter what Boy George said, as long as Boy George said it.

As George's iconic currency went through the roof, so he began to sense the inevitable signs of a back-lash. Out here in consumer land his response to this looked suspiciously like the result of a persecution complex. As rivals threatened his supremacy, and critics made themselves known, George turned hostile. The Durans, the Frankies and the Whams all felt the sarcastic lash of O'Dowd's dangerous tongue. In a series of open letters to the music papers, he let fly bitterly at anyone who'd derided him in print in recent weeks; Steve Severin (of Siouxsie And The Banshees) and Peter Burns (Dead Or Alive) were just two of those who would never walk again. As a guest on Radio Four's Monday morning chat show *Start The Week* the ungracious idol hurled abuse at a caller who dared to suggest that, rather than promoting individuality, George had simply succeeded in spawning another army of clones. Even Jean Rook flinched at his fury, perhaps regretting the sycophancy with which she had rubbed up against the drag megastar earlier in the show. After all, George was the kind of man Ms Rook would normally have subjected to sneering abuse, if he hadn't been a media darling. Approval from the ghastly Jean. Now that, George might have done well to reflect, really *was* the price of fame.

When Culture Club's third album explored the neuroses of celebrity, it came as no great surprise. *Waking Up With The House On Fire* indicated an isolated and besieged Boy George, turning his vanity away from the public whose mores he'd comforted and teased, and inwards towards himself. The LP's cover design had him done up like a '40s screen goddess, a far cry from the child-like waif's visage which so appealingly graced the cover of *Kissing To Be Clever*. All traces of innocence, real or concocted, had been purged, and replaced by mock-Masai female figurines dancing on blazing dollar signs. The same symbol hung in diamante from the ears of the embattled superstar who glowered, narrow-eyed, from the cardboard cover, a grande Hollywood dame risen from the grave. As an emblematic device, the pilfered genre could scarcely have been better chosen.

Compared to what had come before, the contents of *Waking Up* sounded tired and forced. Every hook came overdressed, giving the formally delicate Culture Club sound an almost bombastic edge. There weren't as many perfectly plagiarised melodies as before. The subject matter of the songs was more obliquely articulated than ever, not so much pretending to coy self-reference, as just no-nonsense self-obsessed. Lectures on the pain of being a sensation, mingled with uncomfortable experiments (*Crime Time, Hello Goodbye*), profound melancholia and, in *The War Song*, a clear attempt to match the mammoth impact of Frankie Goes To Hollywood's eruptive *Two Tribes*. George had proclaimed *his* anti-war song to be better because it was 'emotional' (and dreams, remember, were made of emotions). In truth it simply transformed the idea of genocide into a bland platitude of the type *Two Tribes* had managed to avoid becoming, and its failings were heightened by a video drawing strongly on the kind of Nazi chic send-ups Mel Brooks so richly enjoys. To make a comedy of a catastrophe requires that the catastrophe is taken seriously; and the style, context and trappings of *The War Song* smacked more of Boy George feeling himself to be under attack than anything else.

The People failed to warm to Culture Club's new clothes. As a consummate salesman of his own impassioned superficiality, Boy George had been a delightful and unpretentious maker of useful mischief. Now, attempting to go beyond the deliciously fraudulent goals he'd so smoothly attained in his group's first two years at the top, he simply undid the magic of the spell. Released as a 45, the track *Mistake Number Three* became their first commercial failure. The stress-free idealism of their first flush of success was drowned in anxiety and displays of video kitsch which only aped what had gone before. *Waking Up* survived for one week astride the UK album chart during '84's Xmas rush before being displaced, ominously, by Wham's *Make It Big*.

So, what next for the ultimate cuddly toy Boy? George had come closer than anyone else to salvaging lost pop formulations and reviving them for the present day. But that same updated formulation's failings then threatened his very *raison d'être*. Where could he possibly go from a victory so sweet and complete? By changing his tack he would destroy the perfection. By staying the same, his audience eventually just became bored. By framing himself as a complete public relations performer, George made it tough for himself to survive and sustain on the strength of a voice and songs alone. With the Arif Mardin produced *From Luxury To Heartache* making only moderate waves in 1986, it adds strength to the theory that in today's pop arena to become a sophisticated spectacle is essential. But to become a spectacle is also to rely on a decidedly finite resource.

Boy George has made a lot of very attractive running in what is ultimately a pessimistic pop decade. Can the neatest of them all re-invent himself and take centre stage once more? Or is this really goodbye Boy George, not so much a multi-media drama as a cruelly overkilled epic commercial break?

16

::

MADONNA
The Meaning of the Material Girl

What are we going to do about Madonna? Is she Lucifer's revenge for Julie Andrews? or just Nancy Reagan's Freudian flipside in disguise? Should we chastise her for her wicked, wicked ways, or say thank-you for sharing just a slither of her so obvious feeling of delight?

When it comes to Ms Madonna Ciccone a lot of people are unnerved and others are confused. The only thing that's certain is that the little girls understand; and so, of course, does their gleeful blonde-rinsed icon herself. By all the saints, she's got some front! 'My favourite button is my belly button,' said Madonna to the man from *Penthouse* magazine; 'I have the most perfect belly button: an inny, and there's no fluff in it. I never wore a jewel in my belly, but if I did it would be a ruby or an emerald, not a diamond. When I stick my finger in my belly button, I feel a nerve in the centre of my body shoot up my spine. If a hundred belly buttons were lined up against a wall, I could definitely pick out which one is mine.

What a forward girl she is, this Madonna Louise Vernon Ciccone, errant Catholic daughter from the fringes of Detroit; and what a very smart one too. After all, when you sit down and think about it, just what has Madonna got? Er, not an especially marvellous singing voice. Not much of a songwriter's gift, and not too many epoch-making thoughts. But she has got a belly button worth bellowing about. And it was when she took to constructing a career around it that the Earth began to move. Love it or despise it, Madonna is a living, breathing, flourishing example of how to make your assets work.

Back in 1984, Madonna was just another white girl doing nicely out of disco. She had a couple of hits, including two small ones in the UK – *Lucky Star* and *Holiday*. Her eponymous debut album was an unspectacular affair; regulation, radio-conscious funk which asked us tritely to the dancefloor, rhymed 'attraction' with 'reaction' and tended to leave things pretty much at that. More interesting was the cover artwork: a weird and sulky white girl pretending to be secured by a chain around her neck. It was some variation on this personality angle that she needed most of all. *Like A Virgin* set the tone, and with *Material Girl* Madonna found she'd really come up with the goods.

What, in the whole wide world, is more persuasive to a punter than a paradox going public? When Madonna threw herself into the part written into *Material Girl* she expressed the distillate of a modern woman's self-image built on contradictions vast and befuddling enough to scramble even the mind of Gloria Steinem. The

Ms Madonna Louise Vernon Ciccone, superstar and Material Girl.

fascination with Madonna was that she didn't seem to care. She put two and two together and came up with ninety-nine, seventeen, eleven-and-a-half. . .anything but four. In her entire way of carrying on, she claimed the best of all possible options for herself, mixed them up together and didn't *worry* if the pieces didn't match. She liked them that way, and that was good enough for her. Who was going to tell her she was wrong?

Within the ample scope of *Material Girl*, we found ourselves wooed by a winsome siren who was flirtatious yet independent; who was 'feminine' but tough; who could take boys or leave them, but who most of all liked to relieve them of their cash. Her manner said she was an adventurer, but what a pragmatist as well! Whether you considered her a Boy Toy or a tigress, a harlot or a heroine, suddenly Madonna was, above all else, impossible to contain for long inside any of the regular sorts of drawers.

All roads led directly to the navel. It seemed to radiate non-compatibles in every direction at once. What did it mean that she so blithely waved the thing around? 'When I was growing up I remember liking my body and not being ashamed of it,' Madonna told the lady from *Time*; 'I remember liking boys and not feeling inhibited. I never played little games; if I liked a boy, I'd confront him.'

While, on the other hand:

'From when I was very young, I just knew that being a girl and being charming in a feminine sort of way would get me a lot of things, and I have milked it for everything I could.'

And what about:

'Crucifixes are sexy because there's a naked man on them.'

Good God!. . .or maybe Good Godless. Positively sexy or negatively sexist? 'A lot of what I am about is just expressing sexual desire, and not really caring what people think about it,' said Madonna with a shrug. But was the button on display for Madonna's satisfaction or the boys'? Maybe the essence of Madonna is that it's so hard to decide.

As she steamed to the front of the field in 1985, Madonna came to personify the latest variation on a train of post-Punk mixed morality which found its first home in Sting, discovered a benign echo in Michael, a cruder one in Frankie, and a sharper one in Prince. Odd, elusive creatures, all are comprised in differing combinations of love, lasciviousness, lunacy, romance, ruination and most of all an absolute unbending determination to win, win, and win again. 'I won't be happy,' Madonna was reported to have remarked in the *Star* (16/7/85) 'until I'm as famous as God.' Normally we'd assume they'd made it up. This time. . .maybe not.

Madonna gives off the intoxicating scent of someone pursuing their grail with a singular drive and certainty which is as terrifying as it is magnetic. Possessed of a fearsome energy and a forceful, perfectionist nature, we'd describe her as 'gung ho' if she'd just stop scoffing popcorn all the time. A get-ahead female, weaned half on the assumption of emancipation and half in the company of nuns, she has blossomed in an era of trenchant American neo-conservatism. When set within this context, is it so surprising that she should aggravate both bastions of traditionalism and radical crusaders all at once? The Moral Majority consider her depraved and want her to be censored, if not banned. Feminists say she's set the movement back by thirty years, and wish she'd go away. Madonna, predictably enough, doesn't seem to give a toss. She's a self-made business woman, a disciplined, self-contained, all-round performer who knows that the *way* you go about things, as much as what those things are, is the key to modern acclaim. A creature of many, conflicting and renewable dimensions, she works them for all they're worth, projecting her high-intensity persona through every pose, every quote, and almost every public act.

Madonna has steered a hard, straight, unflinching line into the heart of an entombed American past whose whiff of corruption and shame has faded with the passage of time and allowed it to become romantic once more. Madonna gives us Marilyn Born Again, but this time there are no mysterious evil forces pulling puppet or purse strings. Marilyn we remember as a victim. Madonna we celebrate as a survivor. When she recreated the gown and gasping guys which adorned the melting Marilyn who sang *Diamonds Are A Girl's Best Friend* it was a tribute, but only part turned back the clock. Marilyn's song had savvy, but she had to be a good girl to get the precious stones. The Madonna of *Material Girl demands*; and if she doesn't get, she just walks away. It's hard to imagine the Mob blackmailing *her*. 'I,' said Madonna proudly after the soft porn magazines published pictures from her past, and a sleazy soft porn movie bubbled up from the mire, 'am not ashamed of anything I've done.'

In her insolence, and in her relentless chase for eternal glam acclaim, Madonna personifies a new hybrid American showbiz dream whose first true modern manifestation came with Alan Parker's movie *Fame*. Here was an English director providing for the Yanks the nearest they could get to what the British had with post-Punk. *Fame* gave them star-spangled kids of every race and class, not shrugging and complaining and criticising, but punishing themselves to make it in the system. They were caring, sharing people too – almost sickeningly so when they hit the small screen later on – helping each other through Growth Periods, and all that sort of stuff. But mostly, they were scratching, and biting to get into the big game, battling for a piece of immortality's spoils. No existential angst; no change-the-world stuff; no motivation problem; no questions asked. Little Jeffrey Archer would have been proud.

Fame spawned the leg-warmer generation, a slump time, early teen species with no conception or experience of youth culture as an *alternative*, questioning sort of thing, but as a go-for-it, fight-for-it, survival-of-the-fittest career option involving vatloads of sweat and considerable pain. *Fame* was free enterprise and free expression running, jumping, singing and dancing hand in hand. *Fame* was leisure capitalism carpet-bagging the counter culture's Me Generation hangover, liberal America's last gasp before complete capitulation.

Madonna represents a real life Kid From Fame. There's no doubt about it, and no doubts about herself. Madonna takes no drugs because energy and confidence she's got oodles of already. 'I'm pretty forward, I'm not inhibited,' she said. Madonna is fizzy and dizzy but utterly in control. She is aerobicised to bodily magnificence, but stuffs herself with garbage food, and smokes. She's a baby but a grown-up, a bitch with a heart of gold, a stylised reprobate in see-thru clothes and a crucifix, who pretends to jerk off on stage and says she fears the Lord. She's a feminist who isn't, a conservative who's not. Madonna has an angle on everything; 'I thought nuns were really beautiful. For years I wanted to be a nun. I saw them as really pure, disciplined. . .people. They had these really serene faces. Nuns are sexy,' she declared. So too was underwear: 'I have to wear a bra, I'm the only one in my family with breasts. Bras that open in front are best, and torpedo bras are the sexiest. On my *Like A Virgin* record cover. . .I'm in my basque. Basques are very restricting. They have ribs that make you feel you're suffocating and zip up the back. I wear them because they're very 19th centuryish. They have that really svelte look. I like the way it makes my body look. It's very sexual. I wish I was flat-chested so I didn't have to wear a bra. It's one piece of extra clothing to worry about.'

How, you have to wonder, would the Kennedy boys have coped? 'If I had to change my name,' said sacriligious Ms Madonna, 'I'd use my confirmation name Veronica. I chose her because she wiped the face of Jesus which I thought was really dramatic!'

It's drama, drama, drama all the way. *Like A Virgin*? What a cheek! Here it was, the first Madonna tune to really make sense in terms of the overall plot, a song detailing a state of chasteness from a girl who plainly no longer retained it, who sported the name of the woman most pure, yet who didn't mind the man from *Penthouse* knowing she was on the Pill. Could they really be true after all, those myths about convent girls?

Like A Virgin boasted a bountiful, bumping disco backbeat, and a lyric about attaining a feeling of absolute renewal. It was the title track of an album featuring Herself on the cover (in her basque, of course) glowering at us from under her eyelids, perched on the side of a bed, attired in a plunging kind of frock. Here was a picture whose smouldering subject plainly declared 'I'm ready'. But were the rest of us?

Well if our wallets always ruled our emotions we would have resisted her like mad. Only three songs out of ten mattered tuppence between them. *Like A Virgin* was already in the charts, and *Material Girl* and *Into The Groove* weren't far behind. It's this unholy threesome which between them mark the corners of Madonna's magic triangle, defining and bolstering an American phenomenon more worshipped for her extra-musical aura than what's pressed into the plastic. *Like A Virgin* mischieviously taunted taboos, *Material Girl* sealed her exquisite profile, and *Into The Groove* directed us straight to *Desperately Seeking Susan* and what is without doubt Madonna's saving grace.

Though cast and put together before Madonna became the name of '85, *Desperately Seeking Susan* tied in perfectly with her unstoppable surge to the top. *Into The Groove* played a part in the soundtrack, and was billed as such on the album's sleeve notes. The song-and-movie tie-in enabled Madonna to be the perfect subject of a perfect closed promotional circle, typical of modern pop times. The film featured the record. The record was promoted by a video, and the video comprised fast-cut preview clips, lifted from the film and stuck together again. The single, the movie and the booming Madonna persona thus effectively sold not just themselves, but each other as well, every time either the big screen, small screen or phonographic items were witnessed or consumed.

Aside from all this, though, *Desperately Seeking Susan* afforded us a variation on the Madonna palaver which we had not encountered before, and one which banished to the background much that had previously seemed facile about her. Directed with pace and verve by the talented young Susan Seidelman, and featuring the excellent Rosanna Arquette as co-star, the Material Girl played a role with which we were largely familiar from her pin-up pics and songs, but which also differed in particular, vital ways.

Desperately Seeking Susan is a crisp comedy adventure of female friendship and juggled identities which is either feminist or not depending on what kind of feminist you are. . .or aren't. Whatever, Madonna as Susan coloured in a piece of herself which defied the solid jailbait message sent out by the de-contextualised snippets used to make that porny promo for *Into The Groove*. Rather, we see her as a character of genuine and profound independence who sticks loyally by her friends when it comes to the crunch, who likes to tease suburban man's soggy mentality, not his sloppy sexuality, and seeks to damage none but those who seek to damage her. She has little respect for people's privacy, but a lot more than pious types who would proclaim such a virtue for themselves; and when her invasions uncover real pain,

What are we going to do about Madonna?

she responds with sympathy. All in all, a nerve-wracking, but pretty OK kind of girl.

Where does this leave us with Madonna in relation to her fellow female travellers? Pop women since Punk have pursued two general directions, both of them guarded and ambivalent in the face of depressed times. One is towards a cool, demure, career-minded classicism. Along this road we find upmarket video-pop diva Annie Lennox, smartened-up bluesy shouter Alison Moyet, and singular hip AOR lounge bar soul mistress Sade Adu. The other path points to fun and sunshine-seeking Top Shoppers like the affable Bananarama, prototype disco dollies Tracie and DC Lee, and the horribly depressing Patsy Kensit. Madonna, naturally enough, has ploughed her furrow right down the middle of all these. Somehow she has melted together the oggle-fodder aspect of the suspected airhead, with the hard-nosed suss of a total madam mogul. It's an image which has won her a massive following of fans, most of whom, to confound her critics thoroughly, are young women and little girls.

What on earth is it that this semi-virginal lack of emulative admirers has warmed to in so genuine and uncluttered a way? What does all that play-acting and footloose irreverence add up to in a flailing adolescent mind? It's a sense of freedom, of limitless horizons, that seems sure. It's also yet another instance of hand-me-down throwbacks to pre-pop glamour such as have sustained and inspired so many contemporary media darlings, the recipients of a pebble dash splattering of hazy archetypes, now free to work their charms without the hindrances of social or historical context. Perhaps also Madonna provides a junior league manifestation of that revitalised Bitch chic headed so imperiously by Joan Collins in her TV role as the astounding Alexis Carrington-Colby. It has become a cliché that modern American life is just a soap opera based on *Dynasty*. But the great cliché about clichés – that they would not be so, if they weren't so plainly true – holds miserably firm, and at first Madonna seemed nothing more than a thoroughly house-trained 'bad girl' tailored for a striking walk-on part.

She really *did* look so obediently like what neurotic American fantasy required: an apocalyptic 'dirty' disco blonde (blondie?), ruder than Cyndi Lauper, with a girlie pout and a come-hither/get-lost way with the boys; more sophisticated teen rebel product; more kitschy designer sleaze for those awful, spineless *Dynasty* radicals to rub themselves up against; more of that self-loving brand of mind-and-body politics that Californians call progress. Yet where Joan Rivers or her cantilevered namesake, for all their winning venom, represent the New Right's revenge for Women's Liberation – Camp as cop-out instead of righteous defence mechanism – Madonna, at least the one revealed in *Susan*, differs in that she revels in the possibilities of life, while the others are consumed with loathing for it. The media Madonna plays the game for fame, but she plays it too for laughs.

Once you spot the comedy shining through, this lewd and lacy lady becomes a rather different brew. *Like A Virgin*, which had looked like desecration disco with a handsome beat, now looks like a shout of triumphant fulfilment with a handsome beat. *No-one* felt *this* confident when making their break with chasteness. But that's the joke. The point is that she was sad and blue; but now she's celebrating feeling shiny and new. *Into the Groove* meanwhile is just *It's My Party* with claws instead of tears, and *Material Girl* remains a delighted satiric, impudent survivor's anthem. Hear it for a punchline that rescues Madonna from the seamiest attitudes of the other '80s amoralists. While Alexis is a parodic Thatcherine in drag, Madonna at her best is a smarter kind of clown; and in times like these there are worse kinds of sinners to wish you could be like.

CONSUMER GUIDE
– A Definitive Subjective Selection

1) THE POLICE

Long Players

Regatta De Blanc (A&M, 1979): Mainly notable for the presence of impossibly attractive singles *Message In A Bottle* and *Walking On The Moon* which effectively sealed the Police's rise to marketability and credibility too – who would have thought it? *The Bed's Too Big Without You* ploughed a similar furrow – lots of light, shade and appealing self-pity, an emotion invoked throughout the rest of an otherwise variable collection. See also *Bring On The Night* and *Does Everyone Stare.* Your correspondent worked in a West End record shop the Christmas this came out. Hoards of Yuppies in the making writhed with anxiety at the counter – should they buy *Regatta*, the Pretenders' debut or the new MOR Pink Floyd?

Synchronicity (A&M, 1983): After one duff LP and one deeply pretentious one, this was almost a comeback. Forget the narcissistic Jungian rubbish, Andy Summers' ghastly Freudian confession (*Mother*), and the ecological 'message' song on side one. Instead, sink without shame into the flip's lavish love-hate trilogy. You can get *King Of Pain*, *Wrapped Around Your Finger* and *Every Breath You Take* as individual 45s, but as a segue they are devastating. Sting as Sting is a lot more convincing than Sting as hip Social Democrat.

Singles

Fortress (A&M, 1985): Ha! Pushed out as the second 45 from the Blonde One's first solo album *The Dream Of The Blue Turtles*, we learn that Sting, not unlike many greater artists than he, has but one useful thing to say which he says very well. He explores the grey area where passion and possession overlap better than anyone else. The best song on the pretty iffy *Turtles*, it is, ironically given the prestigious array of young jazz talent employed, also the one which sounds most like a single by the Police.

Russians (A&M, 1985): Sting tells us far more as a sexual politician than as a 'social issue' one. Buy this and hear the most fatuous, mock-innocent 'concerned' pop song since *I'd Like To Teach The World To Sing.*

Feature Films

Quadrophenia (Who Films, 1979. Dir. Franc Roddam): Mod-era morality tale, and very good it is too. Sting plays the idealised Ace Face, a mythological inverse to Phil Daniels' desperate, deluded Jimmy. In his first scene, the Policeman rolls up on the

149

Brighton sea front riding the grooviest scooter in town. In his second – cool jerking to the Kingsmen's immortal *Louie Louie* – we see a man transformed from a Wally to an Icon before our eyes. Mod theory into celluloid practice in a handful of frames, the bloody smart alec.

Brimstone & Treacle (Namara Films, 1982. Dir. Richard Loncraine): Nasty, unnerving Dennis Potter-scripted tale of a boy child prone to psychotic bouts of pure malice. Originally made for TV, but banned by the BBC three days before its planned transmission date, it gave Sting his first starring role; and who can deny that he was perfectly cast? When you hear (let alone see) him sing *Spread A Little Happiness*, you just know he's lying through his teeth. That's stardom for you.

Videos
Invisible Sun (Derek Burbidge, 1981): Something else the BBC wouldn't let us see, which just goes to prove what a sorry bunch of fainthearts they are. An entirely passive production, it features painstakingly 'balanced' footage of children and soldiers on the streets of Belfast. The track, taken from *Ghost In The Machine*, is one of Sting's less facile social observation compositions.

Every Breath You Take (Godley & Creme, 1983): Imperious, perilous and predatory desire song, portrayed half as monochrome jazz age spoof, but mostly as subliminal stained glass confessional; the artist as bleeding madonna in drag. Phew.

Wrapped Around Your Finger (Godley & Creme, 1983): See above, but add about a thousand candles and a pure white pyjama suit. Highly effective. Graham Greene would understand.

2) WHAM!
Long Players
Fantastic (Innervision, 1983): Confirming the arrival of the dancing rebel beach party boys, *Fantastic* contains an inferior version of *Wham! Rap!*, plus *Young Guns*, (*Go For It!*), the deeply embarrassing *Bad Boys* and the epoch-definitive *Club Tropicana*. The holiday snap encrusted inner sleeve says more about Wham than cash ever can – almost.

Make It Big (Epic, 1984): Having Gone For It, the Whams said it all with the title of this, their second greatest hits collection at $33\frac{1}{3}$. There was just no arguing with these boys.

Singles
Wham! Rap! (Innervision, 1981): The original, blasphemous and best.

Videos
Club Tropicana (Duncan Gibbons, 1983): A thinly-disguised commercial for Club 18-30.

3) EURYTHMICS
Long Players
Sweet Dreams – Are Made Of This (RCA, 1983): From cover to cut-off, the immaculate middle-tech, middle-brow post-Punk pop conception.

Touch (RCA, 1983): See above, except with diminishing purity, especially on side two. The first half, though, is D&A in their prime.

Singles
Sex Crime (Virgin, 1984): Back into the nightmare world for Alice and her slave with this extract from the basically dispensable soundtrack to *1984*. Ms Lennox is seen to be splendidly fitted for the movie's striking 'prole' outfits. Note appearance of blonde barnet.

Videos
Sweet Dreams (Chris Ashbrook, 1983): Eurythmics-think in moving dot-to-dot visuals. Ms L is most alluring.

Love Is A Stranger (Mike Brady, 1983): Annie throws off her curls. America reels.

Here Comes The Rain Again (Jonathan Gershfield, 1983): Lennox as a storm-tossed Brontë heroine. Stewart as a video camerman. Talk about modern times!

Who's That Girl (Duncan Gibbons, 1984): Meryl Streep and Marilyn make famed bit-part appearances in Swinging London spoof of many hair-pieces. Only a star can get away with videos like these.

Angel (Eddie Arno and Markus Innocenti, 1985): *Be Yourself Tonight* was an uninspired album, with only this cut really seizing the finer feelings of yore. It's a great promo though, sending up the song's own exaggerated prettiness a treat. Absurdism in action, and where else can the video possibly go?

4) MADNESS
Long Players
One Step Beyond (Stiff, 1979): Skulduggery is the key note here, and it makes an incredible contrast with what we expect of Madness today. That edge of *Clockwork Orange* malignance, which has maintained a symbolic presence, was here almost celebrated in both songs – like *Razor Blade Alley* and *In The Middle Of the Night* – and in the only slightly nerve-wracking Nutty Boy dance steps of the then Chas Smash on the back of the cover. On the other hand there was the great loopy comedy of *Night Boat To Cairo* and the title track. And there was *My Girl* – a glimpse into the future.

7 (Stiff, 1981): World-weary, downbeat, deadpan compassion delivered with panache and confidence. All Madness's LPs are worth hearing, but this one introduced them to their place in history.

Keep Moving (Stiff, 1983): More cryptic, but also more streamlined than ever – a relief after the slight over-earnestness of the previous *The Rise And Fall*. *Michael Caine* is a conundrum which still manages to say what it means; *Victoria Gardens* captures faded grandeur with ear-tweaking excellence; and *One Better Day* makes me sniffle.

Mad Not Mad (Zarjazz, 1985): Simply a superb, continuing refinement of everything that's magnificent about these far from *Yesterday's Men*. Its relative commercial failure is a sign of the times, but the fact that they can still sell out a tour make the charts after six years in the forefront of pop is an indication that these people count in a world beyond showbiz. A mighty, mighty band.

Complete Madness (Stiff, 1982): All the hits up to and including 7, plus the breathless, mischievous *House Of Fun*. Sixteen songs that speak volumes for themselves.

Singles
Tomorrow's Just Another Day (Stiff, 1982): A bitter-sweet jauntiness makes this song about futility extra attractive. A less complicated moment from *Rise And Fall*.

Our House (Stiff, 1982): See above, but add a hint of breakdown and suicide. Mercilessly brilliant.

Videos
Complete Madness (Dave Robinson 1979-1983. Released by 'Stiffilms', 1983): Thirteen Madness videos covering early primitive efforts right through to highly sophisticated comic pieces like *House Of Fun, Shut Up* and the matchless *It Must Be Love*.

Tomorrow's Just Another Day (Dave Robinson, 1983): Giant furry dice, prison cells and Suggs McPherson's incredible dancing eyebrows.

Our House (Dave Robinson, 1983): Great mad rubber inflatables make the front room go bananas!

Uncle Sam (John Mills, 1985): The Bomb comes to suburbia and now nobody minds who's swinging on their gate.

5) SPANDAU BALLET

Long Players
True (Reformation, 1983): The first album where Spandau were finally able to deliver the polished leisure-and-lifestyle sound they had always had pretensions to. The title track gave them a huge hit. *Gold* became the anthem to the 1984 Olympic Games, and *Communication* and *Lifeline* provided them with further hits. Very smooth, very 'tasteful', and devoid of any semblance of soul.

Singles
To Cut A Long Story Short (Reformation, 1980): Their first, club-footed 45, containing that Mod ideology-literate line about being young and lovely and free from unsightly grime. Pop culture as pop culture.

Chant Number 1 (Reformation, 1981): Yes, their first decent record, a pastiche of proper dancefloor funk motion that almost holds its own. Beggar & Co. horns help.

Only When You Leave (Reformation, 1984): The spirit of Tony Bennett is alive and well, and haunting a Spandau Ballet melodrama featuring themselves.

Videos
To Cut A Long Story Short (Brian Grant, 1980): Kilts and epaulettes and, yes, they really did look 'very, very young' indeed.

Lifeline (Steve Barron, 1983): Bright spark Barron who did *Beat It* for Michael Jackson, several classics for the Human League, and later directed the computer romance movie *Electric Dreams* here captures the Spands modelling the post-Brideshead country squire look that would later feature heavily in *Next For Men*. Note how the boys have started grinning at each other in that self-congratulatory fashion that is now their indelible trademark.

Communication (Chris Springhorn, 1983): Pop stars playing at James Bond. A classic example of how promos began celebrating the mere fact of their subjects' stardom. Worst of all they don't let us in on the secret of the Black Magic box. Or is it all because the lady loves Milk Tray?

6) DURAN DURAN
Long Players
Rio (EMI, 1982): the quintessential Duran epic, featuring Nagel's painting (Los Angeles!), Malcolm Garrett's graphics (London!) and photography by Andy Earl (Nottingham!). Nine jet-setting numbers include the rapacious, exhilarated hits *My Own Way, Hungry Like A Wolf* and the title track, plus the one that put Sri Lanka on the map, the ballad *Save A Prayer*. Holiday snaps broken up with sleazoid horror cuts *Lonely In Your Nightmare*, and *The Chauffeur*. Roxy Music were never like this.

Singles
Planet Earth (EMI, 1981): The porky, space fantasy debut.

Girls On Film (EMI, 1981): Repulsive piece of gang-bang voyeurism, which also, sadly enough, showed how the Durans *can* play with a good deal of true funk appeal. Shame they haven't got anything compassionate, witty or even especially intelligent to put with it.

Is There Something I Should Know? (EMI, 1983): At last! Paranoia!

Videos
Duran Duran (Various directors, EMI Vision, 1983): A collection of the first eleven Duran promos. As you might expect from essentially pampered, empty-headed young men, the repertoire mixes naive excitement with varying degrees of revolting behaviour. Very pretty in places, very crass in others. Watch out for sea spray.

Dancing On The Valentine (Various directors, EMI Vision, 1984): A trio of social breakdown neurosis vids. *Mad Max* and militarism and all that stuff.

Books
The Book of Words (Edited by DeGraaf and Garrett, Omnibus Press, 1984): One of several DeGraaf/Garrett books, this one, with its Foreword by Simon LeBon, and reproduction of all his song lyrics up to and including *The Wild Boys* tells us a great deal about what makes the operation's imagination tick. LeBon's remarks are most illuminating, and though most of the reporting enclosed is very definitely fan fodder only, here is a volume worth investigating.

7) PAUL WELLER
Long Players
Café Bleu (Polydor, 1984): Style Council LP debut, filled with that blend of

idealism, over-enthusiasm and heavily disguised humour that make our Paul one of my favourite pop people. A flawed experiment – but what a pleasure to discover that romance is not yet dead.

Our Favourite Shop (Polydor, 1985): A more harnessed, less imitative Council sound emerges here, as do some strong songs and good grooves. The blunt-instrument politicking which can undermine the intelligence which inspires it, is leavened with a recurrent sense of poignance. Sterling contributions from DC Lee and comic ace Lenny Henry. The sleeve pic gives us more than a glimpse of Mick and Paul's eloquently English pop cultural roots. It's educational, folks!

Singles
Speak Like A Child (Polydor, 1983): Aching, optimistic, swirling romance. Luverly.

Money-Go-Round (Parts I & II) (Polydor, 1983): Dot-to-dot political worldview on the back, but it still adds up to pretty much perfect sense. Inside, clattering agit-funk without an embarrassment factor. A-minus.

A Paris (Polydor, 1983): A summer EP containing two Talbot instrumentals, and the very beautiful *Long Hot Summer* and *The Paris Match*. The dreamiest hit of the summer. Tracks that 'will melt me forever', as someone wrote at the time. (She was absolutely right.)

My Ever Changing Moods (Polydor, 1984): Latinate pop shuffle, and wistful in all the right places.

8) HOWARD JONES
Singles
New Song (WEA, 1984): Howard's debut and manifesto. Children be free!

Videos
What Is Love? (Danny Kleinman, 1984): Howard at his cuddliest in gay Paris. Almost an erotic dream.

Publications
Risk: Any of the *Risk* fanzines are essential reading for the Howard connoisseur.

9) MICHAEL JACKSON
Long Players
Off the Wall (Epic, 1981): The first solo Michael album since the heyday of the Jackson Five, and, together with Quincy Jones, he put his finger on the post-Rock generation's need for junior aerobic pop. A hatful of spring-heeled hits enclosed. Consumerism as pop-art. Seven million sales worldwide.

Thriller (Epic, 1983): Not since Elvis or the Moptops have so many people been so much in agreement about the virtues of one human being.
(N.B. Also, hear the last decent Jacksons group album, 1980's feel-the-burn nirvana, *Triumph*.)

Singles
They're all on the albums. Why invent when you can recycle?

Videos
Thriller (John Landis, 1983): Early example of the elevation of the promo into a fully-fledged cinema short, with dramatic action, scenario and even plot topping and tailing the song it has been created to showcase. In the future there will be no art. There will only be advertisements.

10) PRINCE
Long Players
Dirty Mind (Warner Bros, 1980): Bedsprings and credulity both at breaking point here as the funk prodigy commences his crossover process in earnest. Musically brilliant, ideologically outlandish, commercially dynamite.

Controversy (Warner Bros, 1981): See above but with the added self-confidence of critical acceptance; and the pretensions. Side one and the bubblegum beauty *Private Joy* are especially recommended.

1999 (Warner Bros, 1983): The stunning title track brilliantly set the scene for Prince's surge to dominant glory the following year, and remains a classic of its time. If you can get hold of the original double package version, it's only worth it for the lewd cover art; all the best tracks appear on the single record version later available in the UK.

Purple Rain (Warner Bros, 1984): Underpinned throughout by acid-headed ecstasy, and ultimately as spineless as it sounds. Moved a few units though, man.

Singles
1999 (Warner Bros, 1983): Dig out the 12-inch if you can't afford the LP.

Kiss (Warner Bros, 1986): . . . almost a loving one, too.

Pop Life (Warner Bros, 1985): From the curious, reactionary, introverted *Around The World In A Day* album, which fits into the Princely game plan as a kind of career/life sequel.

Feature Films
Purple Rain (Warner Bros, 1984, Dir. Albert Magnoli): The mythic version of Prince's life and times set out on celluloid. Not entirely successful, but the 'live' footage is impressive, and as cinematic commercials go, you could do worse.

11) THE THOMPSON TWINS
Long Players
Into The Gap (Arista, 1984): The complete and perfectly packaged guide to modern pop liberalism.

Videos
We Are Detective (Mike Brady, 1983): Very travelling children's repertory, and very Thompson Twins.

12) ELVIS COSTELLO
Long Players
My Aim Is True (Stiff, 1977): Pub rock meets post-modernism. A sulky new songwriting talent is born.

This Year's Model (Radar, 1978): With the correct type of backing sensibility secured, the message is broadened and delivered with sulphurous exuberance.

Armed Forces (Radar, 1979): A supremely confident, ironic and prophetic collection of socio-political epithets. I prefer the wounded subjectivity of the previous effort, but this is still a dandy of a thing.

Get Happy (F-Beat, 1980): After the euphoria, the hangover. The '60s turned inside out and left swinging from their own noose. Not for the squeamish.

Ten Bloody Marys & Ten How's Your Fathers (Imp, 1984): Collection of B-sides, deleted 45s, freebies and alternative takes from the pop phase of Costello's career, which stands as a testament to his astounding hyper-creativity as well as his eclectic talent. Try especially *Girl's Talk* (a hit for Dave Edmunds), *Getting Mighty Crowded* (written by Van McCoy), the odd but evocative *Hoover Factory* and a version of Rodgers & Hart's *My Funny Valentine*; like the performer, a maudlin sensitive thing of timeless attraction.

(NB: all of EC's long players have much to recommend them, especially '83's endlessly rewarding *Imperial Bedroom*. I've limited myself to the albums most relevant to the book here.)

Videos
I Wanna Be Loved ('The Rich Kids', 1984): Never a great lover of the video, Mr EC's caustic, downbeat humour works with simple cleverness on this accompaniment to a 45 lifted from the *Goodbye Cruel World* LP. Why are all these weird people kissing that blotchy man? Watch for yourself and see.

13) THE HUMAN LEAGUE
Long Players
Dare (Virgin, 1981): Ergonomically and aesthetically perfect pop object. The nearest thing yet to a wipe-clean noise.

Singles
(Keep Feeling) Fascination (Virgin, 1982): More logical positivism with a perfect chorus and hook. Love it.

Mirror Man (Virgin, 1982): Graphic art novelty item and all about narcissism. Immaculate.

Life On Your Own (Virgin, 1983): Ah, yes, the most stylised piece of desolation to pop out of the patchy *Hysteria* LP.

Videos
Don't You Want Me (Steve Barron, 1981): See Chapter 13. The key to the whole League puzzle.

(Keep Feeling) Fascination (Steve Barron, 1982): See Chapter 13. The elixir of downmarket Glam charm.

Life On Your Own (Simon Milne, 1983): See Chapter 13. See also Philip's (lack of) hair cut.

Louise (Steve Barron, 1983): See Chapter 13. See also where Virgin boss Richard Branson – the flared-trousered financier – is alleged to live. Is this surrealism?

14) FRANKIE GOES TO HOLLYWOOD
Singles
Relax (ZTT, 1983): Hi-energy, heavy metal, hard funk aural orgasmatron. . .and so on.

Two Tribes (ZTT, 1984): The *Annihilation* 12-inch mix remains the ultimate version of the ludicrous number made available. Though the anti-Frankie backlash had already got under way when this monster of a thing appeared (and God knows, they're far from perfect) I still reckon this gives value for money like few other phonographic discs. It's funny too.

Videos
Relax (Bernard Rose, 1983): The one they banned because of all the bondage. See P. Morley at the start delivering Holly to his 'venue' in a pair of Mickey Mouse ears. See all kinds of things you ain't *never* seen before for that matter – or so they'd like us to think.

Two Tribes (Godley & Creme, 1984): The extended version featuring a bizarre variety of Richard Nixon talking heads, and other caustically scratch-cut politicians is the one to see.

Publications
And Suddenly There Came A Bang (By Paul Morley, ZTT Books): Hard-sell quicky promotional pamphlet in which the journalistic madness of Morley storms the nation's newsagents again. Confused? You will be. Bored? Very possibly. Exploited? Well, it's all in the name of art. Hmm. Contains alleged interview with David Frost.

15) CULTURE CLUB
Long Players
Colour By Numbers (Virgin, 1983): Supreme pop flotsam that melts in the mouth more immediately than probably anything else this decade. Like instant whip it's plagiaristic, transient and slips down a treat. Artificial? Of *course* it is.

Singles
Do You Really Want To Hurt Me? (Virgin, 1982): The distillate of Boy George appeal. Sumptuous.

Videos
Victims (Godley & Creme, 1983): Like all good tittering art students from the pre-Punk era, Godley and Creme understand the camp appeal of Hollywood. So does George. A wholly appropriate treatment for an extremely beautiful song.

Do You Really Want To Hurt Me? (Julien Temple, 1982): Man in frock, in courtroom outrage shock!

The War Song (Russell Mulcahy, 1984): It will take a whole lot more than this to

157

press people into rocking the war boat. A good example of the Boy running out of options.

16) MADONNA
Singles
Lucky Star (WEA, 1984): The first Madonna hit in the UK, a likeable, if unspectacular, slice of disco-pop portraying little of the naughtiness to come.

Like A Virgin (WEA, 1985): Like hell.

Material Girl (WEA, 1985): Ha! The magic potion is complete, and ready to rule the world.

Into The Groove (WEA, 1985): Delectably celebrating *Susan*'s success.

Feature Films
Desperately Seeking Susan (Orion, 1985. Dir. Susan Seidelman): The Madonna persona projected onto the big screen and all the better for it. A very fine movie indeed, proving the divine Ms M to be beyond Punk, beyond Pop, indeed quite beyond a lot of people. The boys are bemused, but the little girls understand.

INDEX